SpeakEasy's

Survival Spanish For Employers

Myelita Melton

SpeakEasy Communications, Incorporated

Survival Spanish for Employers

Author: Myelita A. Melton
Cover illustration: Ellen Wass Beckerman
Published by SpeakEasy Communications, Incorporated
116 Sea Trail Drive
Mooresville, NC 28117-8493
USA

ISBN   0-9786998-2-3

©2006 SpeakEasy Communications, Incorporated. All rights reserved.
No part of this guide may be duplicated or reproduced, stored in a retrieval system, or transmitted, in any form or by any means, electronic, mechanical, recording, or otherwise, without the express written consent of the author.

Survival Spanish for Employers, SpeakEasy Spanish, SpeakEasy's Survival Spanish, SpeakEasy's Survival Spanish for Employers, and SpeakEasySpanish.com are either trademarks or registered trademarks of SpeakEasy Communications, Incorporated in the United States and/or other countries.

The content of this book is furnished for informational use only, is subject to change without notice, and should not be construed as a commitment by SpeakEasy Communications, Incorporated. SpeakEasy Communications, Incorporated assumes no responsibility or liability for any errors, omissions, or inaccuracies that may appear in the informational content contained in this guide.

Foreword

I started learning Spanish at seventeen, and I think it's one of the best decisions I ever made. It happened by accident, but I don't think it was a coincidence. In my senior year of high school I just decided to take Spanish instead of Physics. The sciences were never my thing. On the first day of class, I was hooked. The sound of Spanish spoke to my soul, and I knew I had made the right decision. For the next year I begged my parents to let me take my savings and go to Mexico to study. They thought it was a crazy phase I was going through and it would pass eventually. It didn't. Three days after high school graduation I flew to Mexico for the first time. ¡Muchas gracias, Mom and Dad! Since high school, Spanish has always been a part of my life and it always will be. I'm glad that you are making Spanish a part of your life too.

Spanish hasn't always come easily to me. There have been plenty of times when I couldn't remember the right word— or any word for that matter. I've also made my share of mistakes, and I'm sure I always will. No matter what, I can say that knowing Spanish has rewarded me richly. It's brought me great friends I would never have had, and it's taken me places I would have never been brave enough to go. But best of all, it's given me a greater understanding of Latinos, the most fascinating people on our planet! So, this book is dedicated to you, one of the millions of Americans who want to reach out and make connections with neighbors, friends, colleagues, and customers who speak Spanish. I've loaded it with what I consider to be the essential things that hospitality and service industry professionals should know about one of the most beautiful and expressive languages in the world. ¡Buena suerte, amigos!

Lastly, I'd like to thank to my staff of instructors, proofreaders, artists and editors who catch my mistakes and continue to give me courage. Their time and talents are a constant blessing! Muchas gracias to Ellen Wass Beckerman, Elizabeth Stulz, Candice Tucker, Dr. Leslie Ahmadí, Dr. George Thatcher, Lisa Parker, and Alan Pickelsimer.

Survival Spanish for Employers
Table of Contents

Introduction to Latin America 1

Managing in a Multicultural Environment 2

SpeakEasy's Secrets to Learning Spanish 10

The Sounds of Spanish 12

The Spanish Alphabet 13

The Spanish Accent 14

Pronouncing Spanish Words 14

Spanish Punctuation 14

Spanglish 15

More *Amigos Similares y Familiares* 16

Muchos Ways to *Practicar* 17

Tips & Techniques for *Comunicación* 18

Beginning Words and Phrases 19

Spanish Sounds *Rápido* – What Do I Do Now? 20

Conversaciones to *Practicar* 21

What Is Your Complete Name, Sir? 22

Spanish Nouns 23

A Word about Adjectives 24

The Essentials of Spanish Verbs 25

Acción 26

Sweet 16 Verbs 27

The Big 5 – The Most *Importante Irregulares* 30

Descriptions *Descripciones* 33

Los Números: How Much 34

Days & Months 35

Practicing Numbers and Dates 36

What Time Is It? *¿Qué Hora Es?* 37

Questions Everyone Should Know 38
Getting Information for an Interview 39
The Interview Form 40
The Family – *La Familia* 41
Employee Benefits and Human Resources 43
Employee Motivation 44
Employee Evaluations 46
Discussing the *Problemas* 47
Please Call a Doctor 49
Other Common Problems 50
Workmen's Compensation 51
Insurance 53
Filling Out the Policy 56
Work Clothes 58
Places and Things around the Facility 59
People on the Job 61
Office Furniture 62
Instructions 63
The Way to Go 65
Safety is Number One 66
Lockout–Tagout 69
In the Furniture Factory 70
Textile Terms 71
Around Town 74
Words that Work 76
One for the Road 81
Typing In Spanish Using Microsoft Word 83
Practicing What You've Learned 84
About the Author 87

Using This Material

Welcome to ***SpeakEasy's Survival Spanish for Employers*™**. This material is for adults with no previous experience in the Spanish language. Through research and interviews with professionals in the field, we have developed this material to be a practical guide to using Spanish on the job. Where ever possible, we have chosen to use the similarities between English and Spanish to facilitate your success.

Throughout the manual you will find study tips and pronunciation guides that will help you to say the words correctly. In the guides, we have broken down the Spanish words for you by syllables, choosing English words that closely approximate the Spanish sound needed. This makes learning Spanish more accessible because it doesn't seem so foreign. When you see letters that are **BOLD** in the guide, say that part of the word the loudest. The bold capital letters are there to show you where the emphasis falls in that particular word.

At SpeakEasy Communications, we believe that ***communication*** is more important than ***conjugation***, and we urge you to set realistic, practical goals for learning. Make practice a regular part of your day and you will be surprised at the progress you make!

LATIN AMERICA

What's The Proper Term?
Both!

Latino/Latina: Anyone from Latin America who speaks Spanish as his or her native language. (Preferred)

Hispanic: Anyone who speaks Spanish as his or her native language and traces family origin to Spain.

Note: Don't assume that because a person speaks Spanish that they are Mexican. They could be from anywhere in Latin America

Hispanics in America come mainly from the following three countries:

1. Mexico
2. Cuba
3. Puerto Rico

According to US Census:

1. There are over 43 million in the US, who speak Spanish.
2. Hispanics are the majority minority in America.
3. By 2050 Hispanics will make up 25% of the US population.
4. Georgia & NC have the fastest growing Hispanic populations.
5. Over 17% of the nation's school-aged children are Latino.
6. Latino buying power surged this year to over 700 billion dollars. In 2007 it is expected to increase to over 900 billion dollars.
7. 47% are limited in English proficiency.

Many Latinos from El Salvador, Honduras and Guatemala are coming to America because of Hurricane Mitch in 1998.

Managing in a Multicultural Environment

Effective management and training in a multicultural environment requires at least a basic knowledge of your employee's culture and traditions. Familiarity with both is essential because each has a bearing on a person's every day behavior on and off the job. Where you come from doesn't matter where heritage is concerned. Everyone feels very strongly about it because it's a unique part of our background. Our cultural identity helps us feel like we are "part" of the society around us. It keeps us from feeling isolated and sometimes it helps us know how to react. As Americans, we know it's appropriate to stand when we hear *The Star Spangled Banner* because it's part of our culture. Traditions involving family, religion, education, and nationalism play a large role in any employee's attitude towards professional life. Personal appearance, ethics, and etiquette are also factors to be considered. Whether we realize it or not, culture and tradition are powerful principles we carry with us daily. It's almost like carrying a cell phone. We take it for granted that our phone is in our pocket, but we don't realize it until it rings. Culture is very much like that. It's always with you even though you are unaware of it. Then you hear or see something that rings your cultural bell. That's when culture and tradition can make even the most level-headed person make very emotional decisions.

Even though it's hard to make broad generalizations about culture, many studies have been conducted over the years on its importance to Latin Americans. There are certain basic principles about Latin American culture and tradition that make good survival skills for American employers. This section outlines some of the most ***importante***.

La Familia: The first cultural principle employers should examine carefully is the importance of family. An intense love of family is a strong feature in Latinos. Nuclear families are the foundation of Hispanic society. To most, the family and its needs are more important than work. Working is often seen as a "necessary evil" done for the purpose of earning enough money to satisfy the needs of the family with some left over for the really important things in life: enjoying the company of family and friends. Work should be enjoyed during daylight hours. That leaves quality time in the evening to spend with family. Most Latin Americans prefer not to take the job home because it intrudes on family life. For most employers, this is hard to understand and accept. This is specially true when an employer wants to promote a Latino employee and finds that they prefer to remain in a position that will give them time with family in spite of the pay increase added responsibility brings. Many say that Americans live to work and work to live. Most managers put in hours of overtime and go to work on weekends. For managers in American companies, work even intrudes on vacation time since many of us take business calls when we are off and take time daily to check our email. Latinos prefer to separate their family lives from their business lives and don't want work to be intrusive into what is really important—*la familia*.

La Structura: The structure of typical Latin American families is also different from most American families. Almost always the father is the undisputed head of the household. He makes all major family decisions. In US most family decisions are shared between husbands and wives.

Next let's consider *los niños*. Children in Latino families are cherished, protected and loved. A typical weekend is spent enjoying time together, preparing meals, visiting friends, or extended family. Children are more heavily influenced by their parents and extended family members than by those outside the family. In some cases American kids are more profoundly influenced by their peers or the media than they are by their parents. American children also tend to be more independent at a younger age. We want to raise our children to "stand on their own two feet," whereas many Hispanic parents  concentrate on raising their children to be strong members of their extended families. The family is more important than the individual.

As managers we must also take into consideration the fact that many Hispanic employees have left members of their families behind to take jobs in the United States. This is a sad and complicated fact that occurs for a variety of reasons. Average wages in Latin America are often no more than pennies per hour, not nearly enough to provide basic necessities. In many countries infrastructure is woefully inadequate, and poverty is overwhelming. Often electricity and clean water in the home is still a luxury. Children leave school to go to work so they can help their families. According to the US Census in 2000, 27% of Hispanics over the age of twenty-five had no more than a ninth grade education. Low wages and poverty lead to poor healthcare, lack of good nutrition and a sense of desperation that we can't understand. ***Personal sacrifice is the rule, not the exception.*** The estrangement and isolation that comes with being separated from parents, wives and children can be devastating. This causes severe depression, isolation and even substance abuse. Each of these becomes high risk factors for on the job accidents.

La Religión: Religion and spirituality are also deeply rooted in Latin American culture. Almost 90% Latin Americans are Roman Catholic and most observe basic religious traditions such as baptisms, first communion, marriages and funerals, even though they might not attend church on a regular basis. Throughout Latin America religious practices play a more visible role in the workplace than they do in the US. Anywhere south of the US border it isn't uncommon to see a religious image displayed in a prominent place at work. A priest might also be called in to bless a new building or business endeavor. Many Hispanic managers feel these practices make a valuable contribution to overall worker morale.

An unusual feature of Latin American spirituality is an indefinable fatalism or ***fatalismo*** which is pervasive in the culture. Many Latinos have the underlying sense that their lives are controlled by fate; consequently, whatever success or tragedy befalls them is no result of their own actions. There's no point in being competitive because whatever happens will happen. ***Qué será será***. This is almost opposite of the American belief that our success or lack of it depends solely on the choices we make and the hard work we put into it.

Nacionalismo: Nationalism is deeply ingrained in Hispanics. This is a fact that most Americans don't realize fully. When we see a person speaking Spanish, we automatically assume that the person is Mexican. Often that just isn't true. Spanish is spoken over a wide area that includes eighteen very different countries. If the person comes from a country other than Mexico, this assumption is extremely offensive. All of us are deeply proud of our roots. Latin Americans have deep attachments to their homelands and the unique culture that comes with that. Because you speak English, would you like to be mistaken for a Canadian instead of an American? Probably not! It's savvy management for employers to know which countries their employees come from. Getting to know individual employees is a basic feature in successful Latin American management strategies. The boss becomes personally acquainted with each employee and knows a bit about his family. This is called *personalizmo*, and it's very important to workplace attitudes. When *el jefe* or *el supervisor* recognizes an individual employee, he feels more respected and valued. That increases his loyalty to the company and to its leadership.

Many Americans don't realize how truly different each Latin American country is. People from Venezuela don't enjoy the same taste in foods as those from Peru or Bolivia. Everyone doesn't like *jalapeños* and spicy dishes. There's also a wide variety in music and even fashion.

Los Acentos: As you begin to study Spanish, it's also important for you to realize that how *español* is spoken in each country is different too. Accents and some vocabulary can shift from place to place. That shouldn't be surprising to Americans since our accents change from region to region.

Obviously, people who live in Atlanta speak English differently from those who live in Brooklyn. The same can be said of Spanish. Regional accents are common, but it's still *español*. The differences between Latin American lifestyles and language make Hispanic heritage extremely rich. The culture is as colorful and complicated as any on earth. It is the Spanish language and a few core principles that bind Latinos into a cohesive group. Understanding and appreciating the *diversidad* in Latin America is the key to truly understanding its culture.

La Etiqueta: Basic etiquette and social skills are also valued by Latin Americans. Good manners are a sign of solid upbringing. Training begins at the home and continues in school. Great emphasis is attached to shaking hands and greeting the staff each morning in the workplace. Not only is this sort of etiquette valued in face to face interactions, it's also a part of good telephone etiquette. In a Latin American's eyes it's rude to "cut to the chase" on the telephone and immediately begin to discuss business without first asking how the person is that you are talking to. Next, to be truly polite you should ask how the family is doing. Etiquette is so important on the job many think *por favor* and *gracias* are the two most important phrases in the Spanish language. These are definitely words that will help you get the job done.

Etiquette is also an extremely important feature in the Spanish language. *Español* is very specific in the vocabulary used to denote personal relationships. Specificity in usage is one feature that makes Spanish such a powerful language. Little is left to interpretation because of added details in vocabulary and description. Spanish is so specific that there are two words in it for "you." First there is *Usted*. It is used when you are speaking with business acquaintances, strangers and most adults. *Usted* inherently shows politeness and respect to others. The word "*tú*" is reserved for close personal friends and members of the family. While Americans jump to informality by using first names almost immediately, this can be interpreted as rudeness in Latin American society. That's because a relationship has not yet been built. In Spanish great emphasis is placed on the use of courtesy titles such as *Señor*, *Señora* or *Señorita*. In Latin America there is a real difference between a *friend* and an *acquaintance*; consequently, in most business situations it is better to address an employee *Señor* or *Señora* followed by his or her last name instead of using a first name only—especially at first. This shows respect for the individual and leads to good morale in the workplace.

La Lealtad: Loyalty and quality of work are other hallmarks of Hispanic employees. Historically, Latin American workers have demonstrated exceptional loyalty to *el jefe* or the boss. *Personalismo* or the "cult of personality" still can play a significant role in staff loyalty. In the past that was often a more important factor than company loyalty which is stressed in American companies. At one time *el jefe* was a very paternalistic sort of figure. He was so important in the lives of Hispanic workers they would often ask his advice even on personal problems. But in Latin American firms this has created some inherent communication problems. Employees only tell *el jefe* what he *wants* to hear and not what he *needs* to hear. American employees "tell it like it is" and "let the chips fall where they may" with no regard for what management wants to hear. Promoting open communication between management and staff is an important factor in integrating a multicultural workforce. As business practices change, the relationship between employees and management change. Now personnel policies and pay greatly influence the Hispanic workforce. A friendly working atmosphere where policies are discussed with employees is also essential. This in turn decreases employee turnover and promotes a positive, safe working environment where workers feel free to discuss even the most sensitive issues.

El tiempo: Time and time management are also concepts where Latin Americans and Americans differ greatly. The Hispanic attitude toward time is often called the "*mañana*" or tomorrow complex. It's taken to mean what ever you need done will not be done today—and it doesn't necessarily mean that it will be done tomorrow either. The day after tomorrow will be just as good! In business this goes back to the premise that you will be told what you want to hear. If you want to hear that your shipment or job will be done tomorrow, that's what you will be told. No one wants to disappoint you or hurt your feelings. You are told what will make you happy. When the job isn't completed as you were told, a good explanation will be given to you that saves face for everyone. That's very important. A time commitment is always a good objective, but it isn't binding. For Americans, who always strive to be on time, love punctuality and believe that everything should run according to schedule, this laid-back style can be interpreted as laziness when in actuality it isn't. This is hard to understand in a workplace where "time is money" and there isn't a second to waste.

Strategies for Success: There's no doubt that America's Hispanic workforce is going to become even more important to our country's economic growth and success. Now that you understand some of the basic attitudes your Hispanic workforce has, it's time to plot a course for your success in a multicultural environment.

1. ***Work aggressively to overcome the language barrier.*** Obviously, this means learning to speak some Spanish. You don't have to be fluent to be successful. Employers who have a basic knowledge of Spanish gain the respect of employees for making the attempt. You re also setting a great example which will encourage your Spanish-speaking employees to learn English. It's also important to remember that employers who learn Spanish will avoid the problem of having a Spanish-speaking employee control all the communication that takes

place between management and staff. Even though it is important to encourage and to promote bilingual employees, you want to be able to understand and participate in any discussion of your firm's employment practices and policies.

2. ***Make every effort to learn about the culture of your employees.*** Learning about culture enables employers to better understand their employees as people. This will help you build the relationships that Latinos value so much. In addition, you will also understand the supervisory techniques that are acceptable and unacceptable to employees from another culture. Use several different strategies to develop cultural understanding. First, become familiar with the employees' culture by asking them to describe life back home. Next, they read about the culture of your employees and contrast it with the American culture. There are many great books available that will help you. See the suggested reading list at the back of this book for more information. The more you understand about your employee's culture and heritage the more you will be able to help them develop an appreciation for American culture. This will help your workforce integrate and develop respect for each other.

3. ***Develop an open culture in your workplace that accepts and appreciates the differences individual employees bring to your organization.*** Help all of your employees recognize and appreciate the differences between cultures. One of the realities of integrating people of different races and cultures is that occasionally racism or prejudice emerges. This creates tension and disrespect within the workgroup. Effective managers address these derisive issues quickly and directly by insisting that all employees be treated with respect and dignity regardless of race or cultural background. Effective managers also create opportunities for supervisors and employees to learn about the culture of their Hispanic employees and to appreciate it. Successful employers also take a proactive role in helping Hispanic employees to adjust to the work environment and making them comfortable with their new job. The extra time you take to make this effort will be well worth it.

4. ***Establish employment policies carefully and communicate them so all employees understand your expectations for appropriate conduct on the job.*** Employment policies must be uniformly enforced with all employees. To be effective, set goals for all employees at the beginning of the employment relationship. Work hour requirements, performance requirements, and conduct are all-important issues to cover.

5. ***As required by law, make every effort to hire employees who have legally entered the country.*** Employers have a legal responsibility to check for proper identification of all employees. Fill out an I-9 form on each employee you hire and keep it on file. Make sure you fully understand the serious consequences you risk by hiring undocumented employees.

6. ***Acknowledge your employees' strong family ties and desire to return home periodically.*** Make every effort to develop staffing that is flexible enough to allow employees to return home for a period of time and then return to the job. Many employees earn money to support families at home and often send most of their earnings back to their family at home. Statistically, this can be as much as 85% of their total wages. Recognizing the importance of family ties and providing time off without penalties when ever possible will create a stronger, more loyal and motivated Hispanic workforce. Insist on open communication by asking for several weeks notice before family leave is taken so you can ensure that efficient operation continues in your organization. This will help you see the absence ahead of time so you can plan for it.

SpeakEasy's Secrets to Learning Spanish

Congratulations on your decision to learn to speak Spanish! This is one of the smartest choices you will ever make considering the increasing diversity in our country. It's definitely a decision you will never regret. You are now among a growing number of America's visionary leaders, who want to build better, stronger relationships with Latin Americans, the fastest growing segment of the American workforce.

Learning Spanish is going to open many doors for you, and it will affect you in ways that you can't even imagine. By learning Spanish, you will be able to work more efficiently and safely in almost every workplace in the nation. In addition, you will also be able to give better customer service by building stronger relationships with new Hispanic customers. And-there's another added benefit. You will raise your communication skills to a whole new level.

As an adult, learning a new language requires a certain mind-set. It takes time, patience, and more than a little stubbornness. Just think about it. You didn't learn English overnight- so you can't expect to know everything about Spanish by studying only a few weeks. Adults learn languages quite differently than children do, but you will still make progress quickly by learning practical words and phrases first.

The secret to learning Spanish is having ***self-confidence and a great sense of humor***. To build self-confidence, you must first realize that the entire learning experience is painless and fun. Naturally, you are going to make mistakes. All of us make mistakes in English! So get ready to laugh, learn, and go on from there.

If you took Spanish or another language in high school or college, you are going to be pleasantly surprised when words and phrases you thought you had forgotten begin to come back to you. That previous experience with other languages is still in your mind. It's just hidden away in a little-used filing cabinet. Soon that cabinet will open up again and that's going to help you learn new words even faster.

But there's another idea you should consider, too. What they told you in the traditional foreign language classroom was not exactly correct. There's no such thing as "*perfect Spanish*," just as there is no "*perfect English*." This leaves the door for good communication wide open!

Español is one of the world's most beautiful and expressive languages. Consider these other important facts as you begin:

- ✓ English and Spanish share a common Latin heritage, so literally thousands of words in our two languages are either *similar* or *identical*.
- ✓ Your ability to communicate is the most important thing, so your grammar and pronunciation don't have to be "*perfect*" for you to be understood.
- ✓ Some very practical and common expressions in Spanish can be communicated with a few simple words.
- ✓ As the number of Latinos in the United States increases, so do your opportunities to practice. Trying to say even a phrase or two in Spanish every day will help you learn faster.
- ✓ Relax! People who enjoy their learning experiences seem to acquire Spanish at a much faster pace than others.
- ✓ Set realistic goals and establish reasonable practice habits.
- ✓ When you speak even a little Spanish, you are showing a tremendous respect for Hispanic culture and people.
- ✓ Even a little Spanish or *poco español* goes a long way!

As you begin the process of learning Spanish, you are going to notice a few important differences. Speaking Spanish might feel and sound a little funny to you at first. Don't worry. This is a completely normal. It's because you are using muscles in your face that English doesn't require. Also, your inner ear is accustomed to hearing you speak English. People tell me it sounds and feels like Daffy Duck is inside your head! Just keep going! With practice and perseverance speaking and understanding Spanish will begin to feel more natural to you.

Many Americans know more Spanish than they realize- and pronounce it perfectly. Look at the list on page four and see how many Spanish words you recognize already. Taking the Spanish sounds you already know and practicing them will enable you to learn new principals of the Spanish language easier and faster. This is a great way to build your confidence.

Amigos Similares y Familiares

Americano	Amigo	Hospital	Español	Doctor
Loco	Hotel	Oficina	Agua	Fiesta
Dinero	Señor	Señorita	Señora	Sombrero
Burrito	Taco	Olé	No problema	Accidente
Nachos	Salsa	Teléfono	Quesadilla	Margarita
Tequila	Tortilla	Bueno	Grande	Mucho
Blanco	Adiós	Gracias	Feliz Navidad	Hasta la vista.
Por favor	Pronto	Sí	Aplicación	Cinco de mayo

The Sounds of Spanish

No se preocupe. One of your biggest concerns about acquiring a new language will be speaking well enough so that others can understand you. ***Don't worry!*** Spanish is close enough to English that making a few mistakes along the way won't hurt your ability to communicate.

Here are the *five* vowel sounds in Spanish. These are the most important sounds in this language. Each vowel is pronounced the way it is written. Spanish vowels are never *silent*. Even if there are two vowels together in a word, both of them will stand up and be heard.

A	(ah)	as in mama
E	(eh)	as in "hay or the "eh" in set
I	(ee)	as in deep
O	(oh)	as in open
U	(oo)	as in spoon

Here are other sounds you'll need to remember. Always pronounce them the same way. Spanish is a very consistent language. The sounds the letters make don't shift around as they do in English.

	Spanish Letter	*English Sound*
C	(before an e or i)	s as in Sam: **cero: SAY**-row
G	(before an e or i)	h as in he: **energía**: n-air-**HE**-ah
H		silent: **hacienda**: ah-see-**N**-da
J		h as in hot: **Julio, HOO**-lee-oh
LL		y as in yoyo: **tortilla**, tor- **TEE**-ya
Ñ		ny as in canyon: **español**, es-pan- **NYOL**
QU		k as in kit: **tequila**, tay-**KEY**-la
RR		The "trilled" r sound: **burro, BOO**-row
V		v as in Victor: **Victor**, Vic-**TOR**
Z		s as in son: **Gonzales**, gone-**SA**-les

The Other Consonants - The remaining letters in Spanish are very similar to their equivalents in English.

The Spanish Alphabet
El alphabeto español

A	ah	J	HO-ta	R	AIR-ray
B	bay	K	ka	RR	EH-rray
C	say	L	L-ay	S	S-ay
CH	chay	LL	A-yea	T	tay
D	day	M	M-ay	U	oo
E	A or EH	N	N-ay	V	vay
F	f-ay	Ñ	N-yea	W	DOE-blay-vay
G	hay	O	oh	X	'a-kees
H	AH-chay	P	pay	Y	ee-gree-A-gah
I	ee	Q	coo	Z	SAY-ta

The Spanish Accent

In Spanish you will see two accent marks. Both are very important and do different things. One of the diacritical marks you will notice is called a "tilde." It is only found over the letter "N." But, don't get the Ñ confused with N. The accent mark over Ñ makes it into a different letter entirely. In fact, it's one of four letters in the Spanish alphabet that the English alphabet doesn't have. The Ñ changes the sound of the letter to a combination of "ny." You'll hear the sound that this important letter makes in the English words "canyon" and "onion."

Occasionally you will see another accent mark over a letter in a Spanish word. The accent mark or "slash" mark shows you where to place vocal emphasis. So, when you see an accent mark over a letter in a Spanish word, just say that part of the word louder. For example: José (ho-**SAY**). These accented syllables are indicated in our pronunciation guides with bold, capital letters.

Pronouncing Spanish Words

The pronunciation of Spanish words follows more regular rules than most other languages. That makes it easier to learn. Here are some tips to remember.

1. Most Spanish words that end with vowels are stressed or emphasized on the *next to the last* syllable.
2. Look for an accent mark. If the Spanish word has an accent in it, that's the emphasized syllable.
3. Words that end in consonants are stressed on the *final* syllable.

Spanish Punctuation Marks

You will see two different punctuation marks in Spanish. First there's the upside down question mark (¿). You will see it at the beginning of all questions. It's there to simply let you know that what follows is a question and you will need to give your voice an upward inflection. It's the same inflection we use in English. Then, there's the upside down exclamation mark (¡). It's there to let you know that what follows should be vocally emphasized.

Spanglish

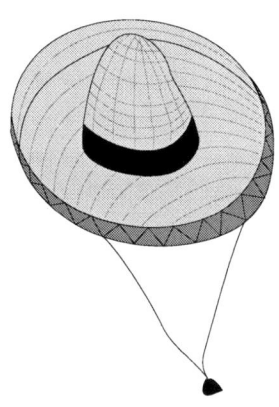

In 1848 the treaty that ended the US-Mexican War signed over much of the Southwest to the United States. This transformed Spanish-speaking Mexicans into Americans overnight! Imagine waking up one morning and finding out you are a citizen of another country. As a result of the treaty, a new language was born that mixes the best of both worlds. Spanglish is a mixture of both our languages. Now, people who use Spanglish span generations, classes and nationalities. It's heard in pop music, seen in print, and used in conversations all through the Americas. Immigrants learning English may turn to Spanglish out of necessity and bilingual speakers use it because it's convenient. Even thought it's still frowned upon in most traditional language classes, it really is a great tool. Listed below are some of our *favoritos*.

Truck/Trocka	Lunch/Lonche	No parking/No parque
Yard/Yarda	Break/Breaka	Cell Phone/El cel

Some English words used as Spanglish are pronounced exactly as they are in English.

El bar	El internet
El break time	La party
El supermarket	La pizza
El email	El record
La dishwasher	El rock-n-roll
El stress	El six-pack

More Amigos Similares y Familiares

Using what you've learned about the sounds of Spanish, practice with the words listed below. Many of the words will be ones you already know or have heard, while others will be new to you. Examine the new words. Some of them will be useful to you at work. Begin by pronouncing each word on the list carefully. After you've pronounced each word, go back through the list again marking the words you can use on the job. Practice these words often to help you remember the basic sounds of español.

Easy Amigos

Carne	Plato	Baño
Tostadora	Rosbif	Bistec
Fruta	Melón	Cantalupo
Contaminación	Temperatura	Champú
Café	Restaurante	Cliente
Fotografía	Supervisor	Compañía
Carro	Problema	Espárragos
Teléfono	Empleo	Familia
Fiesta	Música	Hamburguesa
Banco	Doctor	Hospital
Temperatura	Selección	Hotel
Jalapeño	Instrucción	Identificación
Gasolinera	Metro	Inglés
Farmacia	Museo	Parque
Servicio	Vegetal	Piña
Vacación	Rápido	Pronto
Huevo	Leche	Queso
Pera	Brócoli	Tomate
Agua	Cacerola	Vapor
Patio	Oficina	Vestíbulo
Chocolate	Panqueques	Vinagre
Limonada	Ensalada	Vino

Muchos Ways to Practicar

The more you listen to and use your *español* the easier it will be to learn it. There are lots of great ways to practice that won't cost your any money. Try these practice techniques for improving your skills:

- ✓ Next time you're at a Mexican restaurant, order your food in *español*.
- ✓ Start slowly. Practice one sound each week.
- ✓ Read Spanish language newspapers. They are usually free and easily available.
- ✓ Listen to Spanish language radio stations.
- ✓ Watch Spanish language television via satellite.
- ✓ Rent Spanish language videos, especially cartoons.
- ✓ Buy Spanish tapes and listen to them in the car while you commute.

- ✓ And speaking of tapes, there is such a variety of Latin *música* available, something will be right for you. Listening to music is a great way to train your ears to Spanish and have fun doing it. Personally, I like anything by Carlos Santana or the Salsa of Marc Anthony. What do you like?
- ✓ Visit Internet sites like *http://www.about.com*, where you can find all kinds of information about the Spanish language. They have a wonderful newsletter that comes to you free via e-mail. Most search engines, like Yahoo, have some sort of Spanish section.
- ✓ Next time you listen to a baseball game, keep track of all the Hispanic names you hear.
- ✓ Practice your Spanish every time the opportunity presents itself. This is the only way to get over your nervousness.
- ✓ Try to learn with a friend at work and practice together.

What practice habits work for you?
Share them with us at:
info@speakeasyspanish.com

SpeakEasy's Tips and Techniques for Comunicación

Remember, when you're trying to communicate with a person who is "limited in English proficiency," ***patience is a virtue***! Here are some easy things you can do to make the conversation easier for both of you. For more information on LEP visit this web site: www.lep.gov

- ✓ Speak slowly and distinctly.

- ✓ Do not use slang expressions or colorful terms.

- ✓ Get straight to the point! Unnecessary words cloud your meaning.

- ✓ Speak in a normal tone. Speaking ***loudly*** doesn't help anyone understand you any better!

- ✓ Look for cues to meaning in body language and facial expressions. Use gestures of your own to get your point across.

- ✓ You may not receive good eye contact.

- ✓ Latinos tend to stand closer to each other than North Americans do when they talk to each other, so your personal space could feel crowded. Stand your ground!

- ✓ Feel free to use gestures and body language of your own to communicate.

- ✓ Because of the way languages are learned, it is likely that the person you are talking to understands more of what you are saying, than he is able to verbalize. ***So, be careful what you say!*** No matter what the language, we always understand the bad words first!

Tips & Tidbits
Throughout your book look for the light bulb you see above. This section will give you helpful hints and cultural information that will help you learn easily.

Beginning Words & Phrases

Well, let's get started! In no time you will start gaining confidence. Latinos will be delighted that you are trying to speak *español*. Even if you can't remember a whole phrase, use the words you know. Thank you *gracias* and please *por favor* go a long way toward establishing a rapport.

How many of these common words and phrases do you know?

English	Español	Guide
Hi!	¡Hola!	**OH**-la
How are you?	¿Cómo está?	**KO**-mo ace-**TA**
Fine	Muy bien.	mooy b-**N**
So so	Así así	ah-**SEE** ah-**SEE**
Bad	Mal	mal
Good morning	Buenos días	boo-**WAY**-nos **DEE**-ahs
Good afternoon	Buenas tardes	boo-**WAY**-nas **TAR**-days
Good night	Buenas noches.	boo-**WAY**-nas **NO**-chase
Sir or Mister	Señor	sen-**YOUR**
Mrs. or Ma'am	Señora	sen-**YOUR**-ah
Miss	Señorita	sen-your- **REE**-ta
What's your name?	¿Cómo se llama?	**KO**-mo say **YA**-ma
My name is ___.	Me llamo ___.	may **YA**-mo
Nice to meet you.	¡Mucho gusto!	**MOO**-cho **GOO**-stow
Thank you.	Gracias.	**GRA**-see-ahs
Please!	¡Por favor!	pour-fa-**VOR**
You're welcome.	De nada.	day **NA** da
The pleasure is mine.	El gusto es mío.	el **GOO**-stow es **M`E**-oh
I'm sorry.	Lo siento.	low-see-**N**-toe
Excuse me.	¡Perdón!	pear-**DON**
Bless you!	¡Salud!	sah-**LEWD**
We'll see you!	¡Hasta la vista	**AH**-sta la **VEE**-sta
Good-bye	Adiós	ah-dee-**OS**

Spanish Sounds Rápido – What Do I Do Now?

Be honest! One of the reasons you are hesitant to speak Spanish is that it sounds so fast! Naturally, you're afraid you won't understand. Here are some phrases that will help you. Make learning them a priority. *¿Comprende, amigo?*

English	Español	Guide
I don't understand.	No comprendo.	no com-**PREN**-doe
Do you understand	¿Comprende?	com-**PREN**-day
I speak a little Spanish.	Hablo poco español.	**AH**-blow **POE**-co es-pan-**NYOL**
Do you speak English?	¿Habla inglés?	**AH**-bla eng-**LACE**
Repeat, please.	Repita, por favor.	ray-**PETE**-ah pour fa-**VOR**
I'm studying Spanish.	Estudio español.	es-**TOO**-dee-oh es-pan-**NYOL**
Write it, please	Escribe, por favor	es-**SCRE**-bay pour fa-**VOR**
Speak more slowly, please.	Habla más despacio, por favor.	**AH**-bla mas des-**PA**-see-oh pour fa-**VOR**
Thanks for your patience.	Gracias por su paciencia.	**GRA**-see-ahs pour sue pa-see-**N**-see-ah
How do you say it in Spanish?	¿Como se dice en español?	**CO**-mo say **DEE**-say n ace-pan-**NYOL**
Where are you from?	¿De dónde es?	day **DON**-day ace
May I help you?	¿Puedo servirle?	pooh-**A**-doe seer-**VEER**-lay

The key here is __not__ to pánico.

Your Spanish-speaking employee or friend is having just as much trouble understanding you, as you are having understanding them! Hang in there! Between the two of you, *comunicación* will begin to take place.

SpeakEasy's Conversaciones

Practice Conversation I

USTED:	Good morning, Sir.
SR. GARCÍA	Good morning. How are you?
USTED	Fine, thanks. How are you?
SR. GARCÍA	OK, thanks.

Practice Conversation II

USTED   May I help you? My name is _____.
I speak a little Spanish. What's your name?

SRA. GARCÍA: My name is Carla García Hernandez. I speak a little English.

USTED   Nice to meet you.

SRA. GARCÍA   Yes, nice to meet you.

Can you say the following?

- ✓ Good morning or hi
- ✓ My name is _____.
- ✓ I speak a little Spanish.
- ✓ Do you speak English?
- ✓ Slower, please. Thank you.

¿Cuál Es Su Nombre Completo?
What Is Your Complete Name?

Hispanic Names Have Four Parts

First Name	Middle Name	Father's Surname	Mother's Surname
Primer Nombre	**Segundo Nombre**	**Apellido Paterno**	**Apellido Materno**
Carlos	Jesús	Santana	Rodríguez
José	Pedro	Cuervo	Álvarez
Poncho	Luis	Villa	García
Carmen	Elena	Miranda	Rivera

Start with: Señor,   Señora,   or   Señorita

Use Both Names Or Only The Father's Last Name

Sr. Santana
Sr. Villa

Sr. Cuervo
Sra. Miranda

When A Woman Marries

She Keeps Her Father's Apellido Paterno
She Drops Her Apellido Materno
Last Is Her Husband's Apellido Paterno
Ask for her "Apellido Paterno de Esposo"

Children Have The Apellido Paterno of Both Father and Mother

If Carlos Santana married Carmen Miranda, what is the Nombre Completo of the bebé

José Carlos ???? ?????

Answer: José Carlos Santana Miranda

Spanish Nouns

Can words *really* have a gender?

¡Sí! Spanish belongs to the "romance" language family. It doesn't have anything to do with love, but it has a lot to do with the Romans. In ancient times people had the same trouble learning languages that they do today—except that there were no cassette tapes, CDs, PDAs or very many foreign language teachers. In those days, there weren't many schools for that matter! Consequently, most folks were on their own when it came to learning another language.

To help the difficult process along, words were placed into categories based on how they sounded. This organized the material and made it easier to learn. Old-world languages had many different categories and because the categories were often called "masculine," "feminine," or even "neuter," people began talking about words in terms of their gender. Even though the word "gender" is misleading, the tendency to group words by sound helped people learn new languages more quickly.

Because Spanish evolved from Latin, it has maintained two category divisions for thousands of years. The categories are called masculine and feminine. Even though Spanish can and will evolve, the concept of categories in español is not likely to change.

Here are the most important points to remember about nouns and their categories:

1. Usually, the words are grouped by how they sound, not by what they mean. There will always be a few exceptions!
2. Languages are a lot like the people who use them: They don't always follow the rules!
3. If the Spanish noun is referring to a person, the letter will often indicate the sex of that individual. For example: a doctor, who is a man is a "doctor," while a woman, who is a doctor is a "doctora."
4. Words in the "masculine" category usually end with the letter "O".

NOUN A person, place or thing

5. Words in the "feminine" category usually end with the letter "A".

6. El, la, los and las are very important words. They all mean "the". They are the clues you need to tell you a word's category.

El (masculine category – singular)	El niño, El muchacho
Los (masculine category – plural)	Los niños, Los muchachos
La (feminine category – singular)	La niña, La muchacha
Las (feminine category – plural)	Las niñas, Las muchachas

A Word about Adjectives

In Spanish, most common, descriptive words or adjectives come after the nouns they describe. Conversationally, this is going to require some practice. While you are learning, don't be too concerned about misplacing an adjective or failing to change its final letter to match the noun's category. These are the kinds of common mistakes that everyone makes— even native speakers.

Where the position of adjectives is concerned, there are some notable exceptions. Numbers and other adjectives which show quantity usually come before the noun they describe. That's the way we do it in English!

Descriptive words match the noun by both category and number.

La casa bonita or las casas bonitas

Tips & Tidbits

Always remember that learning the word is the most important thing, not which category it is! When you are trying to say something, small words like "el" or "la" only mean the. They don't give any clues to what you are trying to say to the person that you are speaking with. Learning the fine points of grammar can wait until you are a master of survival Spanish. First, concentrate on learning the words you need to know!

ADJECTIVE Describes a noun

The Essentials of Spanish Verbs

There are basically three types of regular verbs in Spanish. The last two letters on the end of the verb determines how it is to be treated.

Listed below are the three most common types of regular verb endings.

- ✓ AR - Hablar – to speak
- ✓ ER - Comprender – to understand
- ✓ IR - Vivir – to live

In Survival Spanish, we are going to focus on talking about ourselves and talking to another person. That's the most common type of "one on one" communication.

When you want to say I speak, I understand, or I live, change the last two letters of the verb to an "O".

- ✓ Hablo
- ✓ Comprendo
- ✓ Vivo

When asking a question, such as do you speak, do you understand, or do you live, change the ending to an "A" or an "E". The change in letter indicates that you are speaking to someone else.

- ✓ Habla
- ✓ Comprende
- ✓ Vive

To make a sentence negative, simply put "no" in front of the verb.

- ✓ No hablo
- ✓ No comprendo
- ✓ No vivo

VERB — Shows action or state of being

¡Acción!

There are so many English friendly acción words in the Spanish "AR" verb family. Many of them bear a strong resemblance to English verbs- and most of them share a simple, regular nature. They are a very important asset in on-the-job communication. We picked a few of our favorites to get you started. Look closely at the list on page 27. On it, you will recognize many comforting similarities between our languages that are practical too! Changing one letter will really expand your conversational skills.

In on-the-job conversations, people tend to use "I" and "you" to start many sentences. Of all the pronouns, these two are the most powerful and will work the hardest for you. So, that's where we'll start.

Here's an important difference between our languages. In English, the use of pronouns is essential because most of our verbs end the same way. For example, with I speak and you speak; speak remains the same. Our pronouns make all the difference. This isn't true in Spanish. Spanish-speaking people are listening for the letter on the end of the verb. That's what indicates who or what is being talked about. In most cases, you might not hear a pronoun. That's another reason that Spanish might sound a little fast to you: A whole series of words that are important in English are routinely eliminated in Spanish!

Try this: Treat the verbs in the "AR" family as you would "to speak" or "hablar." End the verb with an "o" when you're talking about yourself; "hablo" or "I speak". Change the verb ending from an "o" to an "a" for "habla" or "you speak." Use this form when you're talking to someone else.

English	**Español**	**Guide**
I need	Necesito	nay-say-**SEE**-toe
You need	Necesita	nay-say-**SEE**-ta

**Note: To make a sentence negative, say no in front of the verb. No necesito. No necesita.

The Sweet 16 Verbs

English	Español	Guide
1. To need	Necesitar	nay-say-see-**TAR**
2. To use	Usar	oo-**SAR**
3. To prepare	Preparar	pray-pa-**RAR**
4. To clean	Limpiar	limp-e-**ARE**
5. To work	Trabajar	tra-baa-**HAR**
6. To cook	Cocinar	co-seen-**ARE**
7. To call	Llamar	ya-**MAR**
8. To observe	Observar	ob-ser-**VAR**
9. To inspect	Inspeccionar	een-speck-see-on-**NAR**
10. To ask	Preguntar	prey-goon-**TAR**
11. To carry	Llevar	yea-**VAR**
12. To repair	Reparar	ray-pa-**RAR**
13. To cooperate	Cooperar	co-op-air-**RAR**
14. To empty	Vaciar	va-see-**ARE**
15. To pay	Pagar	pa-**GAR**
16. To return	Regresar	ray-grey-**SAR**

**The "Sweet 16 Verbs" were suggested by participants in SpeakEasy Spanish programs.

Which verbs in the Sweet 16 do you use most often? List your top six:

1. _____

2. _____

3. _____

4. _____

5. _____

6. _____

Now take your top six, change the AR ending to an "a" and make a negative sentence by adding no at the beginning. For example: No necesita. I don't need.

1. _____
2. _____
3. _____
4. _____
5. _____
6. _____

Which verbs would you like to see on the list? Write them below:

1. _____
2. _____
3. _____
4. _____
5. _____
6. _____

Tips & Tidbits

On your journey to Spanish proficiency, make prioritizing your vocabulary your *número uno prioridad*! Go through the "sweet 16" verb list in the table above with different colors of markers. Highlight your "A" list in your favorite color. Look at the vocabulary that remains. Go through it again with a different color- one you don't like so much, and make it your "B" list. Don't begin on your "B" list until you are comfortable with your first choices.

Scenarios

Use verbs from the Sweet 16 to say the following:

1. Use _____

2. Don't use _____

3. Prepare _____

4. I need *(Remember: Pronouns are often eliminated in Spanish)*

   _____

5. Evacuate _____

6. To inform _____

7. I observe _____

8. You observe _____

9. I pay _____

10. I don't pay _____

The Big Five – The Most Importante Irregulares

Now that you have had the opportunity to learn about the tremendous number of verbs that follow regular patterns in Spanish, it's time to take a look at others that don't follow the rules. They are unpredictable, but they are very important. In fact, they reflect some of man's oldest concepts. That's why they tend to be irregular. These words were in use long before language rules and patterns were set. So, here they are: to be (2), to have, to make, and to go. Because they don't follow the rules, you will need to memorize them, but that should be easy because you will use and hear them often.

In Spanish there are two verbs that mean *"to be"*. In English, that's I am, you are, he is, etc. The Spanish version is **ser** and **estar**. **Ser** is used to express permanent things like your nationality or profession. **Estar** is used when talking about location or conditions that change like a person's health.

Ser
Yo **soy**   Nosotros **somos**
Tú **eres**
Él **es**   Ellos **son**
Ella **es**   Ellas **son**
Usted **es**   Ustedes **son**

Estar
Yo **estoy**   Nosotros **estamos**
Tú **estás**
Él **está**   Ellos **están**
Ella **está**   Ellas **están**
Usted **está**   Ustedes **están**

The verb *"to have"* in Spanish is *muy importante*. In English we say that we are hot, cold, hungry, thirsty, right, wrong or sleepy, but in Spanish those are conditions that you have. Some of those expressions mean something totally different than you expected if you get the verbs confused, so be careful!

Tener
Yo **tengo**   Nosotros **tenemos**
Tú **tienes**
Él **tiene**   Ellos **tienen**
Ella **tiene**   Ellas **tienen**
Usted **tiene**   Ustedes **tienen**

In Spanish the verb that means, *"to do"* also means, *"to make."* It's not unusual for one verb to have multiple meanings. There are many expressions that require the use of this verb, but you will use it most when you talk about the weather. That's a safe subject and one that everyone, the world over, discusses! **¿Qué tiempo hace?** What's the weather? **Hace frío.** (It's cold.) **Hace sol.** (It's sunny). **Hace calor.** (It's hot) **Hace viento** (It's windy.). Here's two exceptions: **Está lloviendo.** (It's raining.) and **Está nevando**. (It's snowing.)

Hacer
Yo **hago**   Nosotros **hacemos**
Tú **haces**
Él **hace**   Ellos **hacen**
Ella **hace**   Ellas **hacen**
Usted **hace**   Ustedes **hacen**.

The last of the big five is perhaps the easiest to use. It's the verb that means, *"to go"*. In Spanish, that's **ir**. It's pronounced like the English word ear. Both in English and in Spanish, we use parts of it to make the future tense, in other words, to talk about things that we are going to do. Look at the parts of ir. Then look back at the parts of the verb ser. Do you notice any similarities?

Ir
Yo **voy**   Nosotros **vamos**
Tú **vas**
Él **va**   Ellos **van**
Ella **va**   Ellas **van**
Usted **va**   Ustedes **van**

When you want to say something that you are going to do, start with I'm going or voy. Next, insert the word "a" and the basic verb that states what it is that you're going to do. Try it! It's easy. Here are some examples.

Voy a visitar a mi familia.   I am going to visit my family.
Voy a organizar los trabajadores.   I am going to organize the workers.
Mario va a comprar las plantas.   Mario is going to buy the plants.

**The whole concept of irregular verbs is can be quite daunting. Don't let it defeat you! We have many verbs like this in English. In fact, every language has them. The only way to master them is to practice by using them. Make them your own! Try writing different parts of a verb on your desk calendar. That way, it will be there in front of you every time you look down. When you see it, say it to yourself. Then, you'll have it conquered in no time.

Para Practicar

Using what you've learned in the preceding chapters, write these phrases in español.

1. I am going to work. _____

2. I am going to finish. _____

3. Where is Ramón? _____

4. Where is Carlos? _____

5. I am Tim. _____

6. He is Alan. _____

7. She is Amy. _____

8. I have five sisters. _____

9. He has three brothers. _____

10. Juan has four children. _____

Descriptions or Descripciones

Describing things in Spanish can present problems for English speakers. There are three reasons why this gives us trouble. First, there is the location of the adjective. In English, descriptive words go in front of the noun like white cat, for example. In Spanish, the noun is the most important element, so it comes first (*gato blanco*). However, it gets a little more complicated because there are a few adjectives that are placed before the noun- and they are very common: For example: large or *grande* (*grande gato blanco*). Next, since Spanish nouns are divided into masculine and feminine categories, the descriptive word should match it by category and by number (singular or plural). This leads us to challenge number three: changing the spelling of the adjective. You might need to change a final "o" to an "a" to change the category. Here is a list of descriptive words that can be used in almost any profession.

English	Español	English	Español
Alive	Vivo	**Dead**	Muerto
Good	Bueno	**Bad**	Malo
Better	Mejor	**Worse**	Peor
Big	Grande	**Small**	Pequeño
Clean	Limpio	**Dirty**	Sucio
Hot	Caliente	**Cold**	Frío
Sane	Cuerdo	**Crazy**	Loco
Safe	Seguro	**Dangerous**	Peligroso
Easy	Fácil	**Difficult**	Difícil
Full	Lleno	**Empty**	Vacío
Fast	Rápido	**Slow**	Lento
Hard	Duro	**Soft**	Blando
New	Nuevo	**Old**	Viejo
Rich	Rico	**Poor**	Pobre
Pretty	Bonito	**Ugly**	Feo
Quiet	Tranquilo	**Restless**	Inquieto
Tall	Alto	**Short**	Bajo
Well	Bien	**Sick**	Enfermo
Strong	Fuerte	**Weak**	Débil

Los Números How Much - ¿Cuánto?

Number	Español	Pronunciation Guide
0	Cero	**SAY**-row
1	Uno	**OO**-no
2	Dos	dose
3	Tres	trays
4	Cuatro	coo-**AH**-trow
5	Cinco	**SINK**-oh
6	Seis	**SAY**-ees
7	Siete	see-**A**-tay
8	Ocho	**OH**-cho
9	Nueve	new-**A**-Vay
10	Diez	dee-**ACE**
11	Once	**ON**-say
12	Doce	**DOSE**-a
13	Trece	**TRAY**-say
14	Catorce	ca-**TOR**-say
15	Quince	**KEEN**-say
16	Diez y seis	dee-**ACE**-e-**SAY**-ees
17	Diez y siete	dee-**ACE**-e-see-**ATE**-tay
18	Diez y ocho	dee-**ACE**-e-**OH**-cho
19	Diez y nueve	dee-**ACE**-e-new-**A**-vay
20	Veinte	**VAIN**-tay
21	Veinte y uno	**VAIN**-tay -e-**OO**-no
22	Veinte y dos	**VAIN**-tay -e- dose
23	Veinte y tres	**VAIN**-tay -e- trays
24	Veinte y cuatro	**VAIN**-tay -e- Coo-**AH**-trow
25	Veinte y cinco	**VAIN**-tay -e- **SINK**-oh
26	Veinte y seis	**VAIN**-tay -e-**SAY**-ees
27	Veinte y siete	**VAIN**-tay -e- see-**A**-tay
28	Veinte y ocho	**VAIN**-tay -e **OH**-cho -
29	Veinte y nueve	**VAIN**-tay -e- new-**A**-vay
30	Treinta	**TRAIN**-ta
40	Cuarenta	kwah-**RAIN**-ta
50	Cincuenta	seen-**KWAIN**-ta
60	Sesenta	say-**SAIN**-ta
70	Setenta	say-**TAIN**-ta
80	Ochenta	oh-**CHAIN**-ta
90	Noventa	no-**VAIN**-ta
100	Cien	see-**IN**
200	Doscientos	dose-see-**N**-toes
300	Trescientos	tray-see-**N**-toes
400	Cuatrocientos	coo-**AH**-troh-see-**N**-toes
500	Quinientos	keen-e-**N**-toes
600	Seiscientos	**SAY**-ees-see- **N**-toes
700	Setecientos	**SAY**-tay-see- **N**-toes
800	Ochocientos	**OH**-choh- see- **N**-toes
900	Novecientos	**NO**-Vay-see- **N**-toes
1,000	Mil	meal

Los Días de la Semana y los Meses del Año
Los Días de la Semana

English	Español	Guide
Monday	lunes	**LOON**-ace
Tuesday	martes	**MAR**-tays
Wednesday	miércoles	me-**AIR**-co-lace
Thursday	jueves	who-**WAVE**-ace
Friday	viernes	vee-**AIR**-nace
Saturday	sábado	**SAH**-ba-doe
Sunday	domingo	doe-**MING**-go

It's important to remember when expressing a date in Spanish give the number of the day first followed by the month. Use this format: El (date) de (month).

Los Meses del Año

English	Español	Guide
January	enero	n-**NAY**-row
February	febrero	fay-**BRAY**-row
March	marzo	**MAR**-so
April	abril	ah-**BRILL**
May	mayo	**MY**-oh
June	junio	**WHO**-knee-oh
July	julio	**WHO**-lee-oh
August	agosto	ah-**GOSE**-toe
September	septiembre	sep-tee-**EM**-bray
October	octubre	oc-**TOO**-bray
November	noviembre	no-vee-**EM**-bray
December	diciembre	dee-see-**EM**-bray

Your job starts (*day of the week*) el (*number*) de (*month*).
Su empleo comienza lunes, el 11 de octubre.

Your appointment is Monday the 5th of May.
Su cita es lunes el cinco de mayo.

Practicing Numbers & Dates

Practice these important items by using numbers, days of the week, and months of the year:

- ✓ Your social security number

- ✓ Your driver's license number

- ✓ The numbers in your address

- ✓ Your zip code

- ✓ Your phone number

- ✓ Your birth date

- ✓ Your children's birth dates

- ✓ The dates of holidays

- ✓ License tags of the cars in front of you, when you are stopped in traffic. Combine the Spanish alphabet with this exercise.

- ✓ Phone numbers you see on billboards

- ✓ Numbers found on street signs

- ✓ Phone numbers when you dial them at work or at home

- ✓ The appointments on your personal calendar

- ✓ Your wedding anniversary

- ✓ The dates of all your Spanish classes or practice sessions

¿Qué Hora Es?
What Time Is It?

The concept of time is something that varies from culture to culture. Many countries put less emphasis on being on time than Americans do. For Latinos working in America, this is rapidly changing. They quickly learn the value of ***puntualidad. Es importante!***

Learning to tell time is another good way to put your numbers in Spanish to good use. *¿Qué hora es?* means *what time is it?*

It's one o'clock.	**Es la una.**
It's two o'clock.	**Son las dos.**
It's 3:30.	**Son las tres y media.**
It's 5:45.	**Son las seis menos quince.**

Use the phrases *de la mañana* to indicate morning and *de la tarde* to indicate afternoon. Also midnight is *medianoche*. Noon is *mediodía*.

To find out at what time something takes place ask: *¿A qué hora…?*

¿A qué hora es la reunión?	**What time is the meeting?**
¿A qué hora termina?	**What time do you finish?**

Spanish speakers sometimes use the 24-hour clock for departures and arrivals of trains and flights, etc.

12.05	las doce cero cinco
17.52	las diez y siete cincuenta y dos
23.10	las veinte y tres diez
07.15	las siete quince

Para practicar

1. Using the word for meeting, la reunion, say that the meeting takes place on the hour throughout your regular workday. ***La reunión es a las ocho.***
2. Tell Sr. Rojas what time your store opens and closes.
3. Using the days of the week and the time to explain a work schedule. Your work schedule is…. ***Su horario es…..***

The Questions Everyone Should Know

English	Español	Guide
Who?	¿Quién?	key-**N**
Whose?	¿De quién?	day key-**N**
What?	¿Qué?	kay
Which?	¿Cuál?	coo-**ALL**
When?	¿Cuándo?	**KWAN**-doe
Where?	¿Dónde?	**DON**-day
Why?	¿Por qué?	pour **KAY**
How?	¿Cómo?	**CO**-mo
What's happening?	¿Qué pasa?	kay **PA**-sa
What happened?	¿Qué pasó?	kay **PA**-so
How much?	¿Cuánto?	**KWAN**-toe
How many	¿Cuántos?	**KWAN**-toes

When you ask a question in Spanish, it will take on the same form as a question does in English. Start with the question word that asks the information you need. Follow the question word with a verb, and give your voice an upward inflection.

In Spanish you can also make a question by ending your sentence with ¿no? Here's an example: Cancún está en México, ¿no? When you end a sentence with "no" like this, it takes on the meaning of "isn't it."

The Most Common Questions

How are you?	¿Cómo está?
How much does it cost?	¿Cuánto cuesta?
Where are you from?	¿De dónde es?

Did you notice the upside down question mark (¿) at the beginning of each question? All questions in Spanish begin with this punctuation mark. All exclamatory phrases like, Hi! Begin with an upside down exclamation point like this: ¡Hola! You can do this on your word processor. Refer to "Typing in Spanish with Microsoft Word" in your table of contents for details.

Getting the Información
La entrevista – The Interview

Listed below are the most common questions used during an interview. It's not always necessary to make a complete sentence to have good communication. The information you are asking for is much more important than the phrase "what is your"? As long as you remember to make what you say *sound* like a question by giving your voice an *upward* inflection, people will interpret what you've said *as* a question. Use the form on the following page. Work with a partner to practice giving and receiving information. Make up new answers about yourself for each practice session. You will always be asking the same questions, but the answers you get will always be different!

What's your. . .   **¿Cuál es su. . .**
Coo-ALL ace sue

English	Español
Full name	Nombre completo
First name	Primer nombre
Last name	Apellido
Paternal surname	Apellido paterno
Maternal surname	Apellido materno
Address	Dirección
Apartment number	Número de apartamento
Age	Edad
Date of birth	Fecha de nacimiento
Nationality	Nacionalidad
Place of birth	Lugar de nacimiento
Place of employment	Lugar de empleo
Occupation	Ocupación
Home telephone number	Número de teléfono de su casa
Work telephone number	Número de teléfono de su empleo
Marital status	Estado civil
Driver's license number	Número de licencia
Social security number	Número de seguro social

Información Básica
Imprima por favor

Fecha: _____
                                          Mes   Día   Año

Sr.
Sra.
Srta. _____
        Primer Nombre   Segundo Nombre   Apellido Paterno   Apellido Materno (Esposo)

Dirección: _____
                                    Calle

_____
Ciudad   Estado   Zona postal

Teléfono: Casa _____ **Empleo** _____

             Cel _____ **Fax** _____

Correo electrónico _____

Número de seguro social: _____-_____-_____

Número de identificación de contribuyente (TIN): _____

Fecha de nacimiento _____
                                 Mes   Día   Año

Número de la licencia: _____

Ocupación: _____

Lugar de empleo _____

Estado civil:
- ☐ Casado (a)
- ☐ Soltero (a)
- ☐ Divorciado (a)
- ☐ Separado (a)
- ☐ Viudo (a)

Nombre de esposo: _____
         Primer Nombre   Segundo Nombre   Apellido Paterno   Apellido Materno
Nombre de esposa: _____
         Primer Nombre   Segundo Nombre   Apellido Paterno   Apellido Materno/Esposo

En caso de emergencia: _____ **Teléfono:** _____

Firma: _____ **Fecha:** _____

The Family - La Familia

Family values are extremely important to Latinos. This is something all of us have in common. Many Latinos have left their families in their native countries to come here for economic reasons. No sacrifice is too great for *la familia*.

Children are considered to be precious gifts. Wives, mothers and grandmothers are greatly respected. Remember that all Hispanics have their mother's surname or *materno apellido*. You are going to hear members of the family from your Hispanic customers. It's something all of us like to talk about!

English	**Español**	**Guide**
Aunt	Tía	**TEE**-ah
Uncle	Tío	**TEE**-oh
Brother	Hermano	air-**MAN**-oh
Sister	Hermana	air-**MAN**-ah
Brother-in-law	Cuñado	coon-**YA**-doe
Sister-in-law	Cuñada	coon-**YA**-da
Child	Niño, niña	**KNEE**-nyo, **KNEE**-nya
Cousin	Primo, prima	**PRE**-mo, **PRE**-ma
Daughter	Hija	**E**-ha
Son	Hijo	**E**-ho
Daughter-in-law	Nuera	new-**AIR**-rah
Son-in-law	Yerno	**YEAIR**-no
Father	Padre	**PA**-dray
Mother	Madre	**MA**-dray
Father-in-law	Suegro	soo-**A**-grow
Mother-in-law	Suegra	soo-**A**-gra
Granddaughter	Nieta	knee-**A**-tah
Grandson	Nieto	knee-**A**-toe
Grandfather	Abuelo	ah-boo-**A**-low
Grandmother	Abuela	ah-boo-**A**-la
Husband	Esposo	ace-**PO**-so
Wife	Esposa	ace-**POE**-sa

Para Practicar

Using the verb *tener* (to have), tell your practice partner how many relatives you have in your family. Start like this: ***Tengo*** or I have. Follow that with the number and the member of the family that you are talking about. You will find more about *tener* in the next chapter. Even though it isn't a regular verb, it's very practical. You will use it in many different ways.

En mi familia…..
Write the following sentences in Spanish.

1. I have two sons. _____
2. I have three daughters _____
3. He has four cousins _____
4. My wife has five cousins _____
5. My wife's name is _____
6. I have three uncles _____
7. I have six aunts _____
8. I have no brothers _____
9. I have one (una) sister _____
10. She has no children _____ _____

**In this exercise use the word "mi" for "my."

Employee Benefits & Human Resources
Beneficios y Recoursos Humanos

Go slowly when explaining benefit packages to your new Hispanic employees. The whole concept of tax deductions, insurance deductions, and even overtime could be completely new.

English	Español	Guide
Benefits	Beneficios	ben-nay-**FEE**-see-ohs
Check	Cheque	**CHEC**-kay
Disability	Incapacidad	n-ka-pah-see-**DAD**
Green card	Tarjeta de residencia	tar-**HEY**-ta day ray-see-**DEN**-cee-a
Holidays	Días festivos	**DEE**-ahs fes-**TEE**-vos
Insurance	Seguro	say-**GOO**-row
License	Licencia	lee-**SEN**-see-ah
Medical Insurance	Seguro médico	say-**GOO**-row **MAY**-dee-co
Overtime	Sobre tiempo	so-bray-tee-**M**-po
Paid vacations	Vacaciones pagadas	va-ca-see-**ON**-ace pah-**GA**-das
Paycheck	Paga	**PAH**-ga
Retirement	Retiro or Jubilación	ray-**TEE**-row who-bee-la-see-**ON**
Severance pay	Indemnización por despedida	in-dem-knee-za-see-**ON** pour days-pay-**DEE**-dah
Sick leave	Días pagados por enfermedad	**DEE**-ahs pah-**GA**-dos pour in-fer-me-**DAD**
Social security	Seguro social	say-**GOO**-row so-see-**AL**
Taxes	Impuestos	em-poo-**ACE**-toes
Tax deductions	Deducciones de impuestos	day-dook-see-**ON**-aces day em-poo-**ACE**-toes
Unemployment Insurance	Seguro de desempleo	say-**GOO**-row day dase-em-**PLAY**-oh
Worker's Compensation	Compensación de obrero	com-pen-za-see-**ON** day o-**BRAY**-row

Employee Motivation — Motivación de Empleados

All of your employees appreciate your efforts to encourage and motivate them. This is a great, positive aspect of your position within the company. Doesn't it give you a good feeling to be able to encourage and reward good work with positive comments? Let your Hispanic employees know how much you appreciate their hard work and determination. A big smile will go a long way when you use these phrases.

English	Español	Guide
It's .....!	¡Es....!	es
Excellent	Excelente	x-see-**LEN**-tay
Fantastic	Fantástico	fan-**TAS**-tee-co
Good	Bueno	boo-**WAY**-no
Extraordinary	Extraordinario	x-tra-or-dee-**NAR**-ree-oh
Magnificent	Magnífico	mag-**KNEE**-fee-co
What good work!	¡Qué buen trabajo!	kay boo-**WAYNE** tra-**BAA**-ho
Very good!	¡Muy bien!	mooy b-**N**
You're very important!	¡Usted es muy importante!	oo-**STED** ace mooy m-por-**TAN**-tay
You're very professional.	¡Usted es muy profesional!	oo-**STED** ace mooy pro-fes-see-on-**NAL**
You learn quickly.	Aprende rápido.	ah-**PREN**-day **RAH**-pee-doe
I respect you.	Le respeto.	lay race-**PAY**-toe
You are very valuable.	¡Usted es valioso!	oo-**STED** ace val-ee-**OH**-so
There is…	Hay...	eye
Advancement	Ascenso	ahs-**SEN**-so
Opportunity	Oportunidad	oh-por-too-knee-**DAD**
Great potential	Gran potencial	gran po-ten-see-**AL**
Obvious progress	Progreso obvio	pro-**GRES**-oh ob-**VEE**-oh
Positive Feedback	Reacción positiva	ray-ax-see-**ON** po-see-**TEE**-va
Realistic goals	Metas posibles	**MAY**-tas po-**SEE**-blays

Para Practicar

You are preparing to evaluate one of your best employees who speaks Spanish. What phrases will you use to tell him he does good work and you believe he has potential within your organization? You also want to tell him that is very valuable because among other reasons, he learns very quickly. Write the phrases you need in the space provided below.

1. _____

2. _____

3. _____

4. _____

5. _____

6. _____

Employee Evaluations — Evaluación de Empleados

Helping employees evaluate their job performance helps any business function with better efficiency. Employee performance appraisals occur at regular intervals and are important for both the employee and the employer. The employee should know both strengths and areas that need improvement. After you study this section, review your company's employee evaluation form. Start a form in Spanish to help you prepare for these important conversations.

English	Español	Guide
The company needs to evaluate	La compañía necesita evaluar	la com-pa-**KNEE**-ah nay-say-**SEE**-ta a-val-oo-**ARE**
Goals	Metas	**MAY**-tas
Objectives	Objetivos	ob-hey-**TEE**-vos
Strengths	Puntos fuertes	**POON**-toes foo-**AIR**-tays
Weaknesses	Debilidades	day-bee-lee-**DAD**-aces
Ability	Habilidad	ah-bee-lee-**DAD**
Communication	Comunicación	co-moo-knee-ca-se-**ON**
Control	Control	con-**TROL**
Knowledge	Conocimiento	co-no-see-me-**N**-toe
Language	Lenguaje	len-goo-**AH**-hey
Potential	Potencial	po-ten-see-**AL**
Talent	Talento	ta-**LEN**-toe
The company needs to improve	La compañía necesita mejorar	la com-pa-**KNEE**-ah nay-say-**SEE**-ta may-hor-**RARE**
Production	Producción	pro-duke-see-**ON**
Quality	Calidad	ca-lee-**DAD**
Service	Servicio	ser-**VEE**-see-oh
Operation	Operación	oh-pear-rah-see-**ON**

Discussing the "Problemas"

One of the hardest parts of an employer's job is evaluating employee performance and discussing sensitive subjects. This can be particularly stressful when you are nervous about challenging the language barrier. Before you tackle this situation do some planning first. Think about what you need to say and write a short script in Spanish. Your "cue" cards will help you and give you more confidence. Try not to wait until the last minute to pull this together. The more time that you give yourself to practice, the better your meeting will go. Make sure to save your notes, too. At some point, you may need them again or want to make additions or corrections. Here is a list of words and phrases to get you started.

English	Español	Guide`
There is a problem with your	Hay un problema con su…	ay oon pro-**BLA**-ma con sue
Absences	Ausencias	ow-**SEN**-see-ahs
Using alcohol	Usando el alcohol	oos-**AN**-doe el al-co-**HOL**
Attitude	Actitud	ac-tee-**TUDE**
Conflict	Conflicto	con-**FLICK**-toe
Crime	Crimen	**CREE**-men
Drugs	Drogas	**DRO**-gas
Harassment	Acosamiento	ah-cos-ah-me-**N**-toe
Illness	Enfermedad	n-fair-me-**DAD**
Injury	Trauma	tra-**OW**-ma
Tardiness	Tardanzas	tar-**DAN**-sas
Lack of transportation	Falta de transporte	**FALL**-ta day trans-**POOR**-tay
Lack of English proficiency	Falta de competencia en el inglés	**FALL**-ta-day com-pee-**TEN**-see-ah n el eng-**LACE**
Personal hygiene	Higiene personal	e-he-**N**-ay pear-so-**NAL**
Style of clothing	Estilo de ropa	es-**TEE**-low day **ROW**-pa

English	Español	Guide`
Discrimination	Discriminación	dees-cree-me-na-see-**ON**
Insubordination	Insubordinación	n-sue-bore-dee-na-see-**ON**
Lack of cooperation	Falta de cooperación	**FALL**-ta day co-oh-pear-rah-see-**ON**
Misconduct	Mala conducta	**MA**-la con-**DUKE**-ta
Fight	Pelea	pay-**LAY**-ah

Tips and Tidbits

Employees with different cultural backgrounds will have different attitudes towards work and employers that will have an impact on your management style. According to Eva S. Kras in her book ***Management in Two Cultures*** (Intercultural Press, 1995) Latin Americans are less likely to report an on-the-job injury than American employees. In many areas south of the border workers are essentially trained to tell the boss what he *wants* to hear rather than what he *needs* to hear. Many Latin Americans fear that they will be fired if they become injured on the job— or if they are handling a piece of equipment that breaks. Training is the key to managing these issues. Use your Spanish to help you build open relationships that keep lines of communication open. Making sure that you know everyone's name and how to pronounce it correctly is a good start. In Latin America greeting individual employees is very important

Please, Call a Doctor! - ¡Favor de llamar un doctor!

Even in the safest workplace, accidents are going to happen. Most companies provide first-aid training as a part of the hiring process so that employees know what to do and where to go if they become injured. The following list will help you determine where your employee is hurt.

English	Español	Guide
Ankle	Tobillo	toe-**BEE**-yo
Arm	Brazo	**BRA**-so
Back	Espalda	es-**PALL**-doe
Body	Cuerpo	coo-**AIR**-poe
Brain	Cerebro	say-**RAY**-bro
Chest	Pecho	**PAY**-cho
Chin	Barbilla	bar-**BEE**-ya
Ear	Oreja	oh-**RAY**-ha
Eye	Ojo	**OH**-ho
Face	Cara	**CA**-ra
Finger	Dedo	**DAY**-do
Foot	Pie	**PEE**-ay
Hand	Mano	**MA**-no
Head	Cabeza	ca-**BAY**-sa
Heart	Corazón	core-ra-**SEWN**
Knee	Rodilla	row-**DEE**-ya
Leg	Pierna	pee-**YAIR**-na
Mouth	Boca	**BOW**-ca
Nail	Uña	**OON**-ya
Neck	Cuello	coo-**A**-yo
Nose	Nariz	**NA**-reece
Skin	Piel	pee-**L**
Shoulder	Hombro	**ON**-bro
Spine	Espina	es-**P**-na
Stomach	Estómago	es-**TOE**-ma-go
Throat	Garganta	gar-**GAN**-ta
Toe	Dedo del pie	**DAY**-doe del p-**A**
Tooth	Diente	d-**N**-tay
Wrist	Muñeca	moon-**NAY**-ca

Other Common Problems – Otros Problemas Comunes

Perhaps your employee suffered an on the job accident or has an illness that required time away from work. To ask more in depth questions about the accident and the resulting absence you will need to learn more than the parts of the body. Here is a list of common symptoms and conditions that you will encounter at work.

English	Español	Guide
Abscess	Absceso	ab-**SAY**-so
Blister	Ampolla	am-**PO**-ya
Broken bone	Hueso roto	wWho-**AY**-so **ROW**-toe
Bruise	Contusión	con-too-see-**ON**
Bump	Hinchazón	eem-cha-**SEWN**
Burn	Quemadura	kay-ma-**DO**-ra
Chills	Escalofrío	ace-ca-low-**FREE**-oh
Cough	Tos	toes
Cramps	Calambre	ca-**LAMB**-bray
Diarrhea	Diarrea	dee-ah-**RAY**-ah
Fever	Fiebre	fee-**A**-bray
Indigestion	Indigestión	een-dee-hes-tee-**ON**
Lump	Bulto	**BOOL**-toe
Migraine	Jaqueca	ja-**KAY**-ca
Pain	Dolor	doe-**LORE**
Rash	Erupción	a-roop-see-**ON**
Sprain	Torcedura	tor-say-**DO**-ra
Swelling	Inflamación	een-fla-ma-see-**ON**
Wound	Herido	a-**REE**-doe

Workmen's Compensation

Workmen's Compensation claims are difficult to fill out even when everyone involved speaks English. In many states, Hispanics, especially those in construction, suffer a higher rate of on the job injuries than others. Often this is because of inadequate safety training in Spanish or misunderstandings when work instructions are given. Most Latin American countries do not have workmen's compensation. If a worker is injured on the job, he often loses his position and there is no help with either medical bills or hospitalization. Knowing the parts of the body and the names for common injuries will help you with the process.

English	Español	Guide
Carpentry	Carpintería	car-peen-ter-**REE**-ah
Ceiling installation	Instalación de techos	een-sta-la-see-**ON** day **TAY**-chos
Claim	Reclamación	ray-cla-ma-see-**ON**
Driver	Conductor	con-duke-**TOR**
Deductible	Deducible	day-duke-**SEE**-blay
Driveway	Camino de entrada	ca-**ME**-no day n-**TRA**-da
Electrician	Electricista	elect-tree-**SEES**-ta
Engineer	Ingeniero	n-hen-knee-**AIR**-row
Excavation	Excavación	x-ca-va-see-**ON**
Fall	Caído	ca-**EE**-doe
Injury	Herida	air-**REE**-da
Invoice	Factura	fac-**TOO**-rah
Landscaping	Ajardinando	ah-har-dee-**NAN**-doe
Lifting	Levantamiento	lay-van-ta-me-**N**-toe
Masonry	Albañilería	al-ba-nyee-lair-**REE**-ah
Monthly	Mensualmente	men-sue-al-**MEN**-tay
New construction	Construcción nueva	con-stru-see-**ON** new-wav-**VA**
Paint	Pinta	**PEEN**-ta
Plaster	Yeso	**YEA**-so

English	Español	Guide
Plumbing	Plomería	plo-may-**REE**-ah
Premium	Prima	**PRE**-ma
Residential concrete construction	Construcción residencial de concreto	con-stru-see-**ON** res-see-den-tee-**AL** day con-**CRAY**-toe
Roofing	Techando	tay-**CHAN**-doe
Sales	Ventas	**VEN**-tas
Secretarial	De secretaria	day sec-ree-**TAR**-ree-ah
Sheet metal	Hojalata	oh-ha-**LA**-ta
Swimming pool	Piscina Alberca	p-**SEEN**-ah al-**BEAR**-ka
Tile	Cerámica	say-**RAH**-me-ka
Workman's Compensation	Compensación de obrero	com-pen-sa-see-**ON** day oh-**BRAY**-row

Para Practicar
Circle the correct answer.

1. An *ingeniero* is a. invoice b. deductible c. engineer.
2. An *herida* is a. injury b. ceiling c. secretary.
3. A *prima* is a. driver b. premium c. claim.
4. On the job accidents occur frequently when the following is not done correctly a. Ventas b. Mensualmente c. Levantamiento
5. *Camino de entrada* translates as a. Door b. Driveway c. Roofer
6. *Reclamación* is a. Insurance b. Policy C. Claim

Answer Key: 1. c 2. a 3. b 4. c 5. b 6. c

Insurance — Seguro

Insurance claims and coverage can be a confusing to everyone, but they are especially perplexing to employees from other countries. Only high-level executives in Latin American countries receive benefits. The only benefit that most employees see is a pay check. Prepare your vocabulary carefully when you begin explaining payroll deductions. The concept of having taxes, social security and insurance premiums deducted from one's wages is often difficult to understand. Expect some questions. The following vocabulary will help you explains this puzzling part of American business.

English	Español	Guide
Auto insurance	Seguro de auto	say-**GOO**-row day **OW**-toe
Cancellation	Cancelación	can-say-la-see-**ON**
Clause	Cláusula	**CLOW**-sue-la
Collision	Colisión	co-lee-see-**ON**
Dental insurance	Seguro dental	say-**GOO**-row den-**TAL**
Disability insurance	Seguro de incapacidad	say-**GOO**-row day een-ca-pa-see-**DAD**
Expiration	Expiración	x-pier-rah-see-**ON**
Home owner's insurance	Seguro de hogar	say-**GOO**-row day oh-**GAR**
Hospitalization	Hospitalización	os-pee-tah-lee-sa-see-**ON**
Insurance	Seguro	say-**GOO**-row
Insurance agent	Agente de seguro	ah-**HEN**-tay day say-**GOO**-row
Insurance card	Tarjeta de seguro	tar-**HEY**-ta day say-**GOO**-row
Insurance coverage	Cobertura de seguro	co-bear-**TOO**-rah day say-**GOO**-row
Insurance plan	Plan de seguro	Plan day say-**GOO**-row
Insurance policy number	Número de póliza de seguro	**NEW**-may-row day **PO**-lee-sa day say-**GOO**-row

English	Español	Guide
Insurance premium	Prima de seguro	**PEW**-ma day say-**GOO**-row
Insurance rate	Tasa de seguro	**TA**-sa day say-**GOO**-row
Insured	Asegurado	ah-say-goo-**RAH**-doe
Insured property	Propiedad asegurada	pro-p-a-**DAD** ah-say-goo-**RAH**-da
Life Insurance	Seguro de vida	say-**GOO**-row day **V**-da
Limit	Límite	**LEE**-me-tay
Medical insurance	Seguro médico	say-**GOO**-row **MAY**-d-co
Payment	Pago	**PA**-go
Policy	Póliza	**PO**-lee-sa
Policy face value	Valor nominal de póliza de seguro	va-**LORE** no-me-**NAL** day **PO**-lee-sa day say-**GOO**-row
Policy holder	Asegurado Tenedor de póliza	ah-say-goo-**RAH**-doe ten-nay-**DOOR** day **PO**-lee-sa
Policy requirement	Requisito de póliza	ray-**KEYS**-see-toe day **PO**-lee-sa
Premium adjustment	Ajuste de prima	ah-**WHOS**-tay day **PRE**-ma
Premium default	Incumplimiento de pago de prima	een-coom-plea-me-**N**-toe day **PA**-go day **PRE**-ma
Processing fee	Cargo por procesar	**CAR**-go pour pro-say-**SAR**
Receipt	Recibo	ray-**CEE**-bo
Risk	Riesgo	ree-**ACE**-go
To insure	Asegurar	ah-say-goo-**RAH**-doe

Para Practicar
Match the following

1. _____ Home Owner's Insurance   A. Riesgo
2. _____ Auto Insurance   B. Póliza
3. _____ Policy holder   C. Tarjeta de seguros
4. _____ Premium   D. Seguro de hogar
5. _____ Policy   E. Pago
6. _____ Cancellation   F. Prima de seguros
7. _____ Risk   G. Tasa de seguros
8. _____ Insurance Rate   H. Seguro de auto
9. _____ Payment   I. Cancelación
10. _____ Insurance Card   J. Asegurado

Answer Key: 1. D 2. H 3. J 4. F 5. B 6. I 7. A 8. G 9. E 10. C

Tips and Tidbits
If at all possible, explain the rules and regulations about auto insurance to your employees. Don't take it for granted that everyone understands these complicated rules of the road! Collision and liability coverage are not required in some countries. Also make sure your Spanish-speaking employees understand the importance of having a valid driver's license.

Filling Out the Policy

English	Español	Guide
What is your employer's name?	¿Cuál es el nombre de su empleador?	coo-**AL** es el **NOM**-bray day su m-play-ah-**DOOR**
What is your company's name?	¿Cuál es el nombre de su compañía?	coo-**AL** es el **NOM**-bray day su com-pan-**KNEE**-ah
What is your rate of pay per hour?	¿Cuál es su sueldo base por hora?	coo-**AL** es su **SWELL**-doe **BA**-say pour **OR**-ah
How many hours do you work each week?	¿Cuántas horas trabaja cada semana?	**KWAN**-tas **OR**-ahs tra-**BA**-ha **CA**-da say-**MAN**-ah
When is your next appointment with your doctor?	¿Cuándo tiene su próxima cita con su doctor?	**KWAN**-doe t-**N**-a sue **PRO**-see-ma **SEE**-ta con sue doc-**TOR**
What was the date of your injury?	¿Cuándo era la fecha de su herida?	**KWAN**-dow **A**-ra la **FAY**-cha day sue air-**REE**-da
What is your mailing address?	¿Cuál es su dirección de correo?	coo-**AL** es sue dee-wreck-see-**ON** day co-**RAY**-oh
How many employees do you have?	¿Cuántos empleados tiene?	**KWAN**-toes m-play-**AH**-does t-**N**-a
What is the amount of your annual payroll?	¿Cuál es el total de su nómina anual?	coo-**AL** es el toe-**TAL** day sue **NO**-mee-na an-oo-**AL**
What is your general liability?	¿Cuál es su responsabilidad general?	coo-**AL** es su ray-spon-see-bill-lee-**DAD** hen-nay-**RAL**
Do you have prior coverage?	¿Tiene cubiertos antes?	t-**N**-a coo-bee-**AIR**-toes **AN**-tays
Do you have prior losses?	¿Tiene perdidos antes?	t-**N**-a pear-**DEE**-dos **AN**-tays
Do you work in other states?	¿Trabaja en otros estados?	tra-**BA**-ja n **OH**-tros es-**TA**-does
Who is your general contractor?	¿Quién es su contratista general?	key-**N** ace sue con-tra-**TEES**-ta hen-nay-**RAL**
How many years do you have in business?	¿Cuántos años tiene en negocio?	**KWAN**-toes **AN**-yos t-**N**-a in nay-**GO**-see-oh

English	Español	Guide
What is your federal employer identification number?	¿Cuál es su número federal de identificación para empleadores?	coo-**AL** es su **NEW**-may-row fed-day-**RAL** day e-dent-tee-fee-ca-see-**ON** **PA**-ra m-play-ah-**DOOR**-ace
What is your social security number?	¿Cuál es su número de seguro social?	coo-**AL** es su **NEW**-may-row day say-**GOO**-row so-**SEE**-al

Para Practicar

Señor Carlos Ramírez has come to your office to apply for an insurance policy. Ask him the following questions for your form.

1. What is your social security number?

   _____

2. What is your company's name?

   _____

3. How many years have you been in business?

   _____

Work Clothes— Ropa de Trabajo

Dressing appropriately for the work place is an important part of safety guidelines. You will find that some South American countries don't have clear mandates for work attire. Even American companies vary their safety requirements because of state laws or other concerns. Every company is different, so there's a great need to explain your precise requirements to your employees.

Here is a list of the most common items of clothing and safety items used in manufacturing and distribution.

English	**Español**	**Guide**
Badge	Insignia de identificación	en-**SEEG**-knee-ah day i-den-tee-fee-ca-see-**ON**
Ear plugs	Tampones	tam-**PONE**-ace
Gloves	Guantes	goo-**AN**-tays
Hairnet	Red del cabello	red del ca-**BAY**-yo
No jewelry	No joyas	no **HOY**-as
Pants	Pantalones	pan-ta-**LOAN**-ace
Safety glasses	Gafas de seguridad	**GA**-fas day say-goo-ree-**DAD**
Shirt	Camisa	ca-**ME**-sa
Shoes	Zapatos	sa-**PA**-toes
Uniform	Uniforme	oon-knee-**FOR**-me

Places and Things around the Facility
Lugares y cosas alrededor de la facilidad

It's going to be important for you to conduct new employee orientation. In any orientation a tour of your facility will be essential. Here are some important features found in many facilities. Which of these do you have at your site? Label each in English and Spanish, so every one can learn This will send a clear signal to Spanish-speaking employees that they are very important and valued in your organization.

Do you know any of these terms already?

English	Español	Guide
Bag	Bolsa	**BOWL**-sa
Bath room	Baño	**BAA**-nyo
Box	Caja	**CA**-ja
Break room	Sala de descanso	**SA**-la day des-**CAN**-so
Conveyor belt	Cinta transportadora	**SEEN**-ta trans-por-ta-**DOOR**-ah
Door	Puerta	poo-**AIR**-ta
Elevator	Ascensor	ah-sen-**SOAR**
Exit	Salida	sa-**LEE**-da
Factory/plant	Fábrica	**FA**-bree-
Forklift	Carretilla Elevadora	Car-ray-**TEE**-ya a-lay-va-**DOOR**-ah
	Montacargas	mon-ta-**CAR**-gas
Human resources	Recursos humanos	ray-**COOR**-sos oo-**MAN**-nose
Intercom	Interfono	n-ter-**FOE**-no
Lab	Laboratorio	la-bore-ra-**TOR**-ree-oh
Loading dock	Cargadero	car-ga-**DAY**-row
Locker	Casillero	ca-see-**YEA**-row

English	Español	Guide
Lunch room	Sala de almuerzo Cafetería	**SA**-la day al-moo-**AIR**-so ca-fay-ter-**REE**-ah
Machine	Máquina	**MA**-key-na
Mixer	Batidora	baa-tee-**DOOR**-ah
Mixing room	Cuarto de mezcla	coo-**ARE**-toe day **MES**-cla
Office	Oficina	oh-fee-**SEEN**-na
Pallet	Paleta	pa-**LAY**-ta
Parking lot	Estacionamiento	es-ta-see-on-na-me-**N**-toe
Plastic	Plástico	**PLA**-stee-co
Production	Producción	pro-duck-see-**ON**
Production line	Línea de producción	**LEA**-nay-ah day pro-duke-see-**ON**
Start button	Botón de comienza	bow-**TON** day co-me-**N**-sa
Stop button	Botón de pare	bow-**TON** day **PA**-ray
Water fountain	Fuente del agua	foo-**N**-tay del **AH**-goo-ah

Para Practicar:
Name five places from the list above that you would show new employees in an orientation session.

1. _____
2. _____
3. _____
4. _____
5. _____

People on the Job

In this list you will often see two definitions for the same position. This is because in Spanish there is a small change in spelling when the word used for a man or for a woman. This spelling change isn't as complicated as it sounds, because it only true when you are talking about people. How many job categories from the list below do you have in your organization? Which title is appropriate for your position in the firm? Highlight only job titles you will use at your particular company.

English	**Español**	**Guide**
Line worker	Trabajador de línea	tra-ba-ha-**DOOR** day **LEA**-nay-ah day
Operator	Operador/operadora	oh-pear-ra-**DOOR** oh-pear-rah-**DOOR**-ah
Lead person	La persona que dirige	la pear-**SEWN**-na kay dee-**REE**-hey
	Jefe/jefa	**HEY**-fay / **HEY**-fa
Supervisor	Supervisor Supervisora	sue-pear-v-**SOAR** sue-pear-v-**SOAR**-ra
Plant superintendent	El supervisor de planta	el sue-pear-**V**-soar day **PLAN**-ta
	El director de planta	el dee-wreck-**TOR** day **PLAN**-ta
	El gerente de planta	el hair-**RENT**-tay day **PLAN**-ta
Receptionist	Recepcionista	ray-sep-see-on-**EAST**-ta
Secretary	Secretaria	sec-ray-**TAR**-ree-ah
President	Presidente	pres-see-**DEN**-tay
Director of Human Resources	Director de recursos humanos	dee-wreck-**TOR** day ray-**COOR**-sos oo-**MAN**-nose

Office Furniture — Muebles de la Oficina

Now that you are learning the terms for the places and people in your facility, it's time to take on words for common items in your work space. As a constant reminder to keep working on your *español*, label the following items. Use removable labels so you can see the word each time you look around your office.

English	Español	Guide
Answering machine	Contestador telefónico	con-tes-ta-**DOOR** tay-lay-**FO**-knee-ca
Armchair	Sillón	see-**YOWN**
Bench	Banco	**BAN**-co
Bookshelf	Librero	lee-**BRAY**-row
Calculator	calculadora	cal-coo-la-**DOOR**-ra
Calendar	Calendario	ca-len-**DAR**-ree-oh
Chair	Silla	**SEE**-ya
Computer	Computadora	com-po-ta-**DOOR**-ra
Desk	Escritorio	es-cree-**TOR**-ree-oh
Electrical outlet	Enchufe	n-**CHEW**-fay
File cabinet	Archivo	are-**CHEE**-vo
Lamp	Lámpara	**LAM**-pa-rah
Pen	Lapicero	la-p-**SAY**-row
Pencil	Lápiz	**LA**-peas
Printer	Impresora	eem-pray-**SOAR**-ah
Scissors	Tijeras	t-**HAY**-rahs
Stapler	Engrapadora	n-gra-pa-**DOOR**-rah
Sofa	Sofá	so-**FA**
Table	Mesa	**MAY**-sa
Tape	Cinta engomada	**SEEN**-ta n-go-**MA**-da
Trash can	Cesto de basura	**SEIS**-toe day ba-**SUE**-rah
Window	Ventana	ven-**TA**-na

Tips and Tidbits

Some office supplies just don't translate. That's when you will be glad to know Spanglish. What could these items possibly be? El email, El post-it, el white-out and el-glue-stick

Instructions - Instrucciones

Here are some common instructions for the workplace. Remember to always use the word **instructions** rather than **directions**. This could be confusing to some Latinos because the word *dirección* in Español can mean *address*! It's a good idea to ask this simple question: *¿Comprende mis instrucciones?* Also, don't forget to add *por favor* and gracias to all your *instrucciones*! Then you will really see *resultados!*

English	Español	Guide
Come here.	Venga aquí.	**VEN**-ga ah-**KEY**.
Let's go.	Vámonos.	**VA**-mo-nos
Go with him.	Vaya con él.	**VAY**-ya con **L**
Wait	Espere.	es-**PEAR**-ray
Stop.	Pare.	**PAR**-ray
Help me.	Ayúdeme.	ay-**U**-day-me
Help him.	Ayúdelo.	ay-**U**-day-low
Like this.	Así.	ah-**SEE**
Not like this.	Así no.	ah-**SEE** no
Show me.	Muéstreme.	moo-**ACE**-tray-me
Good.	Bien.	b**N**
Point to it.	Indícalo.	n-**D**-ka-low
Move that here.	Mueve eso aquí.	moo-wavy **ES**-o ah-**KEY**
Bring me that.	Tráigame esto.	try-**GA**-may **ES**-toe
Give it to me.	Démelo.	**DAY**-may-low
To the right	A la derecha.	a la day-**RAY**-cha
To the left.	A la izquierda.	a la ees-key-**AIR**-duh
Remove these.	Quite estos.	**KEY**-tay **ES**-toes
Pick up all these.	Recoja todo esto.	ray-**CO**-ha **TOE**-dos **ES**-toes
Put it there.	Póngalo allí.	**PON**-ga-low ah-**YE**
Around	Alrededor	al-ray-day-**DOOR**

English	Español	Guide
Inside	Dentro	**DEN**-tro
Under	Debajo	day-**BAH**-ho
Carry this.	Lleve esto.	**YEA**-vay **ES**-toe
Turn off	Apague	ah-**PAH**-gay
Turn on	Encienda	n-see-**N**-da
Open	Abre	**AH**-bray.
Close	Cierra	see-**AIR**-ra
Do it now.	Hágalo ahora.	**AH**-ga-low ah-**OR**-ah
Do it later.	Hágalo más tarde.	**AH**-ga-low mas **TAR**-day
Here	Aquí,	ah-**KEY**
There	Allí	ah-**YE**
A little	Un poco	un **PO**-co
A lot	Mucho	**MOO**-cho

Para Practicar

Use the phrases above in combination with the appliances and rooms of the house to say the following:

1. Go with Pablo and help him. _____

2. Bring me that. _____

3. Pick up all these. _____

4. Please, do it now. _____

5. Do it later, thank you. _____

6. Show me. _____

7. Point to it. _____

The Way to Go

The ability to give directions in *español* is one of the most practical skills you can have. It adds to your conversational ability and it's a skill you will use over and over again. Slowly, you can start to learn this important vocabulary by knowing simple things, such as the four directions: north, south, east and west. Then, add turns like right and left. Before you know it, you'll be able to give directions to places around town and in your facility. This is also easy vocabulary to practice because you can work on it anywhere you go!

English	Español	Guide
Where is it?	¿Dónde está?	**DON**-day ace-**TA**
North	Norte	**NOR**-tay
South	Sur	**SUE**-er
East	Este	**ACE**-tay
West	Oeste	oh-**ACE**-tay
Above	Encima	n-**SEE**-ma
Aisle	Pasillo	pa-**SEE**-yo
Avenue	Avenida	ah-ven-**KNEE**-da
Behind	Detrás	day-**TRAHS**
Down	Abajo	ah-**BAA**-ho
Here	Aquí	ah-**KEY**
In front of	En frente de	n **FREN**-tay day
Inside	Adentro	ah-**DEN**-tro
Near	Cerca	**CER**-ca
Next to	Al lado de	al **LA**-doe day
Outside	Afuera	ah-foo-**AIR**-ah
Over there	Allá	ah-**YA**
Straight ahead	Adelante	ah-day-**LAN**-tay
Street	Calle	ca-**YEA**
There	Allí	ah-**YE**
To the left	A la izquierda	ah la ees-key-**AIR**-dah
Turn	Doble	**DOE**-blay
To the right	A la derecha	ah la day-**RAY**-cha
Up	Arriba	ah-**REE**-ba

Safety Is Number One - Seguridad Es Número Uno

Safety is a major concern in every workplace. It's important to realize that some of your Latino employees will be unfamiliar with some of the tools and safety procedures required for the job you're doing. Safety regulations and practices can vary widely from country to country. So making a commitment to training and to good communications can prevent many serious accidents.

Make sure to talk about safety on a regular basis. Check with state and national associations to see if safety materials are available in Spanish. You're going to be pleasantly surprised! Practice these key phrases and the vocabulary that follows.

All safety rules must be obeyed.
Es preciso obedecer todas las reglas de seguridad.

The violation of any safety rule can result in your dismissal.
La violación de cualquier reglamento puede resultar en que se termine.

Be careful.
Tenga cuidado.

You must wear your safety glasses.
Debe que llevar sus anteojos de seguridad.

Hearing protection is required.
Se requiere protección del oído.

Clean this area.
Favor de recoger este area.

Where is your supervisor?
¿Dónde está su jefe? (su supervisor)

English	Español	Guide
Accident	Accidente	ax-see-**DENT**-tay
Barricade	Barricada	bar-ree-**KA**-da
Be careful.	Tenga cuidado.	**TEN**-gah kwee-**DA**-doe
Bruised	Golpeadas	gol-pay-**AH**-das
Burns	Quemadas	kay-**MA**-dahs
Cleanliness	Limpieza	limp-p-**ACE**-ah
Danger!	¡Peligro!	pay-**LEE**-grow
Defect	Defecto	day-**FEC**-toe
Electrocution	Electrocución	a-lec-tro-cue-see-**ON**
Excavation	Excavación	x-ka-vah-see-**ON**
Falls	Caídas	ka-**EE**-das
Fire	Fuego	foo-**A**-go
Fire extinguisher	Extinguidor de fuego	x-ting-gee-**DOR** day foo-**A**-go
First aid	Primeros auxilios	pre-**MAY**-rows aux-**E**-lee-ohs
Fractures	Fracturas	frac-**TO**-ras
Gasoline	Gasolina	gas-oh-**LEAN**-ah
Guardrail	Barandillas	ba-ran-**D**-yas
Hard hat	Casco	**KAS**-co
Harness	Arnés	are-**NES**
Heat exhaustion	Agotamiento de calor	ah-go-ta-me-**N**-toe day ka-**LORE**
High top safety boots	Botas de seguridad bien ajustadas	**BOW**-tas day say-goo-ree-**DAD** **BN** ah-whos-**TA**-dahs
High voltage	Alto voltaje	**AL**-toe vol-**TA**-hey
Ladder	Escalera de mano	es-ka-**LAIR**-ah day **MAN**-oh
Lifting	Levantamiento	lay-van-ta-me-**N**-toe
Maintenance	Mantenimiento	man-ten-knee-me-**N**-toe
No smoking.	No fumar	no foo-**MAR**
Platform	Plataforma	pla-ta-**FOR**-ma
Protection	Protección	pro-teck-see-**ON**
Pulling nails	Sacando clavos	sa-**CAN**-doe **CLA**-vows
Rigging	Sujeción	soo-heck-see-**ON**

English	Español	Guide
Safety belt	Cinturón de seguridad	seen-to-**RON** day say-goo-ree-**DAD**
Safety glasses	Anteojos de seguridad	anti-**OH**-hos day say-goo-ree-**DAD**
Safety glasses	Gafas de protección	**GA**-fas day pro-tec-see-**ON**
Safety vest	Chaleco de seguridad	cha-**LAY**-co day say-goo-ree-**DAD**
Scaffold	Andamio	ann-da-**ME**-oh
Scraped	Raspadas	ras-**PA**-das
Shirt	Camisa	ka-**ME**-sah
Shoring	Apuntalamiento	ah-poon-tal-la-me-**N**-toe
Strained	Distendidas	dees-ten-**DEE**-das
Trench	Zanjas	**SAN**-has

Para Practicar:

¡Tenga cuidado!

1. You need ear protection.
   _____

2. You need eye protection.
   _____

3. You need safety boots.
   _____

4. Where is your hard hat?
   _____

Lockout — Tagout

Below is a list of common lockout/tagout vocabulary. To learn these words and phrases in Spanish, go through the list and highlight the terms you use most often. Look at the pronunciation guide and sound the words out. The bold capital letters indicate the part of the word that receives vocal emphasis.

English	Español	Guide
Lockout Tagout	Cierre y Etiquetado	see-**EH**-ray e eh-t-kay-**TA**-doe
Do not operate	No operar	no oh-pear-**RAR**
Do not start	No arrancar	no ah-rahn-**CAR**
Jammed	Atascado	ah-tahs-**CA**-doe
Manually	Manualmente	man-oo-ahl-**MEN**-tay
Moving parts	Partes móviles	**PAR**-tays **MO**-v-lace
Never ignore tags	Nunca ignore una etiqueta	**NOON**-ca eg-**NOR**-ay **OO**-na eh-t-**KAY**-ta
Normal operations	Operaciones normales	oh-pear-ra-see-**ON**-ace nor-**MAL**-lace
Notify	Notificar	no-t-fee-**CAR**
Off/shut down	Apagado	ah-pa-**GA**-doe
On	Prendido	pren-**D**-doe
One key per lock	Una llave por candado	**OO**-na **YA**-vay pour can-**DA**-doe
Plug in	Enchufar	n-chew-**FAR**
Procedure for shut down	Procedimiento de cierre	pro-said-d-me-**N**-toe day see-**EH**-ray
Remove a lock	Quitar un candado	key-**TAR** oon can-**DA**-doe
Remove a tag	Quitar una etiqueta	key-**TAR OO**-na eh-t-**KAY**-ta
Safety device	Aditamento de seguridad	ah-d-ta-**MEN**-toe day say-goo-ree-**DAD**
Maintenance work	Trabajo de servicio	tra-**BA**-jo day ser-**V**-see-oh

In the Furniture Factory
En la fábrica de muebles

A professor at Amherst College stated recently that *Spanglish* could be traced to the end of the US-Mexican war in 1848 when it transformed Spanish-speaking Mexicans into Americans. So the colorful mixture of English and Spanish that is used on the job across the nation today has an extremely rich heritage. Almost everyone uses it. Look for the *Spanglish* words in the list below. Start listening whenever you hear Spanish spoken for new ones to add to your list.

English	Español	Guide
Arm	Brazo	**BRA**-so
Back	Respaldo	rays-**PALL**-doe
Break	Descanso	days-**CAN**-so
	Breaka	**BREAK**-ah
Chair	Silla	**SEE**-ya
Cushion	Cojín	co-**HEEN**
Cutter	Cortador	cor-ta-**DOOR**
Fabric	Tela	**TAY**-la
Fill	Relleno	ray-**YEA**-no
Frame	Armadura	are-ma-**DOO**-rah
Framer	Framero	fra-**MAY**-row
Furniture	Muebles	moo-**A**-blays
Inspection	Inspección	een-speck-see-**ON**
Leather	Cuero	coo-**AIR**-row
Lunch	Almuerzo	al-moo-**AIR**-so
	Lunche	**LUN**-chay
Machine	Máquina	**MA**-keen-na
Needle	Aguja	ah-**GOO**-ha
Ottoman	Otomana	oh-toe-**MA**-na
Pattern	Diseño	d-**SAIN**-yo
Seat	Asiento	ah-see-**N**-toe
Sew	Coser	co-**SAIR**
Skirt	Falda	**FALL**-da
Sofa	Sofá	so-**FA**
	Couche	**COW**-chay

English	Español	Guide
Springs	Muelle	moo-**A**-yea
Spring-up	Incluye los muelles	een-**CLUE**-yea los moo-**A**-yace
To frame	Hacer la estructura	ah-**SER** la es-truc-**TOO**-rah
To sew on a machine	Coser a máquina	co-**SAIR** ah **MA**-keen-na
Upholstery	Tapicería	ta-p-sair-**REE**-ah

Textile Terms

Even though Spanish and English have many words and phrases in common, in manufacturing or other technical fields, it's not always possible. Many of the products and processes that we take for granted do not exist in Latin America. Take, for example, the common building product "drywall." In Latin America, it just doesn't exist! Now, it's commonly referred to as *el drywall* or *el sheetrock*. There are no rules here! As your Spanish fluency grows and you become more confident, work with your Spanish-speaking employees to find common ground in *Spanglish*!

English	Español	Guide
100%	Cien por ciento	**SEE**-n pour see-**N**-toe
Bird eyes	Ojo de perdiz	**OH**-ho day pear-**DEESE**
Blend	Mezcla or Combinación	**MACE**-kla kom-be-na-see-**ON**
Breaking setups	Romper la instalación	rom-**PEAR** la n-stah-lah-see-**ON**
Break	Pausa	**POW**-sa
Broken needles	Romper una aguja	Rom-**PEAR** una ah-**GOO**-ha

English	Español	Guide
Color	Color	co-**LORE**
Computer	Computadora	com-poo-ta-**DOOR**-ah
Cone	Cono	**KO**-no
Cotton	Algodón	al-go-**DON**
Defect	Defecto	day-**FEC**-toe
Doff	Quitarse	key-**TAR**-say
Drops	Bajadas	ba-**HA**-dahs
Fabric	Tela	**TAY**-la
Fiber	Fibra	**FEE**-bra
Gray	Gris	greese
Heather	Brezo	**BRAY**-so
Hole	Boquete	bow-**KET**-tay
	Agujero	ah-goo-**HEY**-row
Knitter	Persona que hace punto	Pear-**SEWN**-na kay **HA**-say **POON**-toe
Knitting machine	Máquina de tricotar	**MA**-key-nah day tree-ko-**TAR**
Knit wear	Artículos de punto	are-**TEE**-coo-los day **POON**-toe
Lot Number	Número de lote	**NEW**-may-row day **LOW**-tay
Machine	Máquina	**MA**-key-nah
Material	Material	ma-tear-ree-**AL**
Matrix	Matriz	**MA**-treez
Merge Number	Número de unir	**NEW**-may-row day **OO**-near
Natural	Natural	na-too-**RAL**
Needle	Aguja	ah-**GOO**-ha
Needle line	Línea de aguja	**LEE**-nay-ah day ah-**GOO**-ha
Number	Número	**NEW**-may-row
Preparation	Preparación	pray-pah-ra-see-**ON**
Problem	Problema	pro-**BLAY**-ma
Quality	Qualidad	ca-lee-**DAD**
Rags	Andrajo	an-**DRA**-ho
Repacks	Rembalaje	ray-em-bah-**LA**-hey
Roll	Rollo	**ROW**-yo

English	Español	Guide
Scales	Escala	es-**KA**-lah
Set-ups	Preparaciones	pray-par-ra-see-**ON**-aces
Stitch	Punto	**POON**-toe
Tickets	Boleto	bow-**LAY**-toe
To end	Terminar	ter-me-**NAR**
To knit	Hacer punto	ah-ser **POON**-toe
	Hacer malla	ah-ser **MA**-ya
	Tejer	tay-**HAIR**
	Tricotar	tree-ko-**TAR**
To prepare	Preparar	pray-pa-**RAR**
To repair	Reparar	ray-pah-**RAR**
To start	Comenzar	co-mince-**ARE**
Yarn	Hilaza	ee-**LA**-sa
Yarn Count	Cuenta de hilaza	coo-**N**-tah day ee-**LA**-sa

Para Practicar

If you work in a textile facility, list the ten most practical vocabulary words from the list above in the space provided below.

1. _____
2. _____
3. _____
4. _____
5. _____
6. _____
7. _____
8. _____
9. _____
10. _____

Around Town

Spanish-speaking employees may need more than new employee orientation. You may need to help them find places around town where they can do their banking, buy their groceries or mail a letter. Knowing they can count on your for information will help you to provide a more open work environment. This vocabulary will provide you with the kind of terminology that will make you a good ambassador for your company and your city. No one wants to run in circles!

Use the vocabulary from the chapter on directions to practice giving directions to some of the places below. The next time you go out to run errands around your city or town, check the list below. Where are you going? Make a numbered list of the places you intend to go along with the Spanish words for the directions that will get you there. Now you can practice two important sets of vocabulary at the same time. Also think about grouping this vocabulary into logical sets. Which places involve travel? Which places involve recreation? Which locations do your guests ask you about most often? Now, let's get going!

English	**Español**	**Guide**
Airport	Aeropuerto	ah-eh-row-poo-**AIR**-toe
Bakery	Panadería	pan-ah-day-**REE**-ah
Bank	Banco	**BAN**-co
Barber shop	Peluquería	pay-loo-kay-**REE**-ah
Beauty salon	Salón de belleza	sa-**LAWN** day bay-**YEA**-sa
Church	Iglesia	e-**GLAY**-see-ah
City hall	Municipio	moon-knee-**SEE**-p-oh
Fire department	Departamento de bomberos	day-par-ta-**MEN**-toe day bom-**BAY**-rows
Florist	Florería	floor-ray-**REE**-ah
Gas station	Gasolinera	gas-so-lee-**NAY**-rah
Grocery store	Grosería	gros-eh-**REE**-ah

English	Español	Guide
Hospital	Hospital	os-p-**TAL**
Hotel	Hotel	oh-**TEL**
Jewelry store	Joyería	hoy-eh-**REE**-ah
Laundromat	Lavandería	la-van-day-**REE**-an
Library	Biblioteca	b-lee-oh-**TECK**-ah
Market	Mercado	mare-**CA**-doe
Movie theatre	Cine	**SEEN**-nay
Museum	Museo	moo-**SAY**-oh
Park	Parque	**PAR**-kay
Pharmacy	Farmacia	far-**MA**-see-ah
Police station	Estación de policía	es-ta-see-**ON** day po-lee-**SEE**-ah
Post office	Correo	core-**A**-oh
Restaurant	Restaurante	res-tower-**AHN**-tay
School	Escuela	es-coo-**A**-la
Shoe store	Zapatería	sa-pa-tay-**REE**-ah
Store	Tienda	t-**N**-da
Super market	Super Mercado	soo-**PEAR** mare-**CA**-doe
Theatre	Teatro	tay-**AH**-trow
Train station	Estación de tren	es-ta-see-**ON** day tren
Subway	Metro	**MAY**-tro

Para Practicar

Using the list above write down the Spanish names for the places employees ask you about.

_____

_____

_____

Words that Work

Knowing words from the list below will begin to take you from survival Spanish to the next level. This vocabulary is designed to cover a variety of on the job situations where accidents, inspections and investigations are concerned. Each of these areas will require study on your part and advance preparation. As you work on this list, think critically about the problems that are inherently associated with your industry. That's where to start. Work on five words each week until your become comfortable with your entire list. When difficult situations arise, take time to make a quick reference guide. It will help you communicate even in the toughest situations. For further study and vocabulary investigate the OSHA website. At www.osha.gov, you can access several English–Spanish dictionaries which cover a variety of occupational issues.

English	Español	Guide
Accident	Accidente	ax-see-**DEN**-tay
Accident investigation	Investigación de accidente	n-ves-t-ga-see-**ON** day ax-see-**DEN**-tay
Affected employee	Trabajador afectado	tra-ba-ha-**DOOR** ah-fec-**TA**-doe
Appeal	Apelar	ah-pay-**LAR**
Approve	Aprobar	ah-pro-**BAR**
Area inspection	Inspección de zona	n-spec-see-**ON** day **SO**-na
Authorize	Autorizar	ow-tor-ree-**SAR**
Break the law	Quebrantar la ley	kay-brahn-**TAR** la lay
Checklist	Lista de comprobación	**LEES**-ta day com-pro-ba-see-**ON**
Citation	Citación	see-ta-see-**ON**
Combined violation	Infracción combinada	n-frac-see-**ON** com-b-**NA**-da
Complaint	Queja	**KAY**-ha
Compliance	Conformidad	con-for-me-**DAD**
Comply	Cumplir	coom-**PLEAR**
Consult	Asesorar	ah-say-soar-**RAR**

English	Español	Guide
Consultant	Asesor	ah-say-**SOAR**
Consultation	Consulta	con-**SOOL**-ta
Danger	Peligro	pay-**LEE**-grow
Death	Muerte	moo-**AIR**-tay
Demonstrate	Demostrar	day-mo-**STRAR**
Deposition	Deposición	day-po-see-see-**ON**
Develop	Desarrollar	des-ah-row-**YAR**
Discipline	Disciplina	d-see-**PLEA**-na
Discrimination	Discriminación	dees-cree-me-na-see-**ON**
Disease	Enfermedad	n-fer-me-**DAD**
Display	Exhibir	x-e-**BEER**
Division	División	d-v-see-**ON**
Egregious	Flagrante	flah-**GRAN**-tay
Employee	Empleado	m-play-**AH**-doe
Employee medical record	Expediente médico del empleado	x-pay-d-**N**-tay **MAY**-d-co del m-play-**AH**-doe
Employee representative	Representante de los trabajadores	ray-pray-sen-**TAHN**-tay day los tra-baa-ha-**DOOR**-ace
Employer	Empleador	m-play-ah-**DOOR**
Enforce	Imponer	m-po-**NAIR**
Evidence	Evidencia	a-v-**DEN**-see-ah
Exposure	Exposición	x-po-see-see-**ON**
Fact sheet	Hoja informativa	**OH**-ja een-for-ma-**T**-va
Failure to abate	Falta de corrección	**FAHL**-ta day co-wreck-see-**ON**
Fatality	Fatalidad	fah-tal-lee-**DAD**
First aid	Primeros auxilios	pre-**MAY**-rows ow-**SEE**-lee-ohs
First violation	Primera infracción	pre-**MAY**-rah een-frac-see-**ON**
Follow-up inspection	Inspección de verificación	een-spec-see-**ON** day ver-ree-fee-ca-see-**ON**
Hazard	Riesgo	ree-**ACE**-go
Health	Salud	sa-**LEWD**
Health hazard	Riesgo contra la salud	ree-**ACE**-go **CON**-tra la sa-**LEWD**

English	Español	Guide
Hearing	Audiencia	ow-d-**EN**-see-ah
Hygiene	Higiene	e-he-**N**-ay
Illness	Enfermedad	en-fer-me-**DAD**
Imminent danger	Peligro inminente	pay-**LEE**-grow en-me-**NEN**-tay
Implement	Poner en práctica	po-**NAIR** n **PRAC**-t-ca
Improve	Mejorar	may-ho-**RAR**
Injury	Lesión	less-see-**ON**
Inspect	Inspeccionar	een-spec-see-oh-**NAR**
Inspection	Inspección	een-spec-see-**ON**
Inspector	Inspector	een-spec-**TOR**
Interview	Entrevista	en-tray-**V**-stah
Investigation	Investigación	een-ves-t-ga-see-**ON**
To issue	Emitir	ay-me-**TEER**
Law	Ley	lay
Lawyer	Abogado	ah-bow-**GA**-doe
Letter of corrective action	Carta de acción correctiva	**CAR**-ta day ax-see-**ON** co-wreck-**T**-va
Lost workdays	Días laborables perdidos	**D**-ahs lah-bore-**RAH**-lace pear-**D**-dose
Mandatory	Obligatorio	oh-blee-ga-**TOR**-ree-oh
Medical treatment	Tratamiento médico	trah-ta-me-**N**-toe **MAY**-d-co
Noncompliance	Incumplimiento	een-coom-plea-me-**N**-toe
Occupational	Ocupacional	oh-coo-pa-see-oh-**NAL**

English	Español	Guide
Occupational safety and health administration	Administración de seguridad y salud ocupacional	ahd-me-knee-strah-see-**ON** day say-goo-ree-**DAD** y sa-**LEWD** oh-coo-pa-see-oh-**NAL**
Offense	Ofensa	oh-**FEN**-sa
Other than serious violation	Infracción no seria	een-frac-see-**ON** no **SAY**-ree-ah
Owner	Dueño	do-**WAYNE**-yo
Partnership	Asociación	ah-so-see-ah-see-**ON**
Penalize	Penalizar	pay-nal-lee-**SAR**
Penalty	Multa	**MOOL**-ta
Periodic inspection	Inspección periódica	een-spec-see-**ON** pay-ree-**OH**-d-ca
Permanent	Permanente	pear-ma-**NEN**-tay
Permissible exposure	Niveles de exposición permitidos	knee-**VEL**-ace day x-po-see-see-on pear-me-**T**-dos
Place of employment	Lugar de trabajo	lu-**GAR** day tra-**BA**-ho
Poster	Póster	**PO**-stair
Prevent	Prevenir	pray-vay-**NEAR**
Priority	Prioridad	pre-oh-ree-**DAD**
Program	Programa	pro-**GRAH**-ma
Project	Proyecto	pro-**YEC**-toe
Question	Pregunta	pray-**GOON**-ta
Random inspection	Inspección al azar	een-spec-see-**ON** al ah-**SAR**
Reasonable	Razonable	rah-sewn-**NA**-blay
Record	Registro de exposición del empleado	ray-**HE**-strow day x-po-sce-see-**ON** del m-play-**AH**-doe
Reduce	Reducir	ray-do-**SEER**
Referral	Referencia	ray-fer-**WREN**-see-ah
Regulation	Reglamento	ray-glah-**MEN**-to

English	Español	Guide
Repeat violation	Infracción repetida	een-frac-see-**ON** ray-pay-**T**-da
Require	Requerir	ray-kay-**REAR**
Research	Investigar	een-ves-t-**GAR**
Respond	Responder	res-pon-**DARE**
Review	Examinar	x-ah-me-**NAR**
Rights	Derechos	day-**RAY**-chos
Routine inspection	Inspección rutinaria	een-spec-see-**ON** roo-t-**NAR**-ree-na
Rule	Regla	**RAY**-gla
fety	Seguridad	say-goo-ree-**DAD**
Safety hazards	Peligros a la seguridad	pay-lee-**GROWS** ah la say-goo-ree-**DAD**
Serious	Serio	**SAY**-ree-oh
Serious physical harm	Daño físico serio	**DAN**-yo **FEES**-co **SAY**-ree-oh
Serious violation	Infracción seria	een-frac-see-**ON SAY**-ree-ah
Services	Servicios	ser-**V**-see-ohs
Severity	Severidad	say-ver-ree-**DAD**
Standards	Normas	**NOR**-mas
Suspended penalty	Multa suspendida	**MOOL**-ta seus-pen-**D**-dah
Substantial failure to comply	Falta de cumplimiento sustancial	**FAHL**-ta day coom-plea-me-**N**-toe seus-than-see-**AL**
Temporary	Temporal	tem-pour-**AL**
Threat	Amenaza	ah-men-**NA**-sa
Trainer	Entrenador	een-tren-na-**DOOR**
Training	Instrucción	een-struc-see-**ON**
Verify	Verificar	vay-ree-fee-**CAR**
Violation	infracción	een-frac-see-**ON**
Walk around	Recorrido	ray-core-**REE**-doe
Witness	Testigo	tes-**T**-go
Worker	Trabajador	tra-baa-ha-**DOOR**
Working conditions	Condiciones laborales	con-d-see-**ON**-ace la-bore-**RAL**-ace

One for the Road: Phrases to Use Any Time

Obviously, conversation is made up of more than just lists of words. It will take practice and determination for you to achieve free-flowing conversation in a language that's new to you. Learning Spanish is a slow and steady process for adults. It could take several months before you begin to "think" in Spanish, so don't expect to achieve native speaker speed over night! There will be times when you feel like you can't remember anything you've studied. That's natural. It happens to everyone. Try not to be discouraged. The rewards you'll receive from learning to speak Spanish are far greater than a little bit of frustration. If you keep working, it won't be long before you'll have a breakthrough. Learning Spanish is a lot like eating a great steak. You don't want to rush it. Cut each bite of your Spanish, chew it over carefully and savor each morsel. Moving along at a slower pace will help you retain what you learn longer.

Spanish is a language that has loads of zest and flair. It is punctuated with single words and short phrases that can really express a lot of sentiment. The next time you have an opportunity to observe native speakers, listen carefully. You may hear them switch from English to Spanish, depending on what they are saying. And, you might hear them use any of the "one-liners" listed below. Phrases like these add spice to your conversation. Use the following list to help you take your conversational skills to the next level.

English	Español	Guide
Are you sure?	¿Está seguro? (a)	es-**TA** say-**GOO**-row
Excellent!	¡Excelente!	x-say-**LENT**-tay
Fantastic!	¡Fantástico!	fan-**TA**-stee-co
Good idea.	Buena idea.	boo-**A**-na e-**DAY**-ah
Happy birthday!	¡Feliz cumpleaños!	fay-**LEASE** coom-play-**AHN**-yos
Have a nice day.	Tenga un buen día.	**TEN**-ga un boo-**WAYNE DEE**-ah
I agree.	De acuerdo.	day ah-coo-**AIR**-doe
I believe so.	Creo que sí.	**CRAY**-oh kay **SEE**
I'm so glad.	Me alegro.	may ah-**LAY**-gro

English	Español	Guide
I'll be right back.	¡Ahora vengo!	ah-**OR**-ah **VEIN**-go
I'm leaving now.	¡Ya me voy!	ya may **VOY**
That's OK.	Está bien.	es-**TA** b-**N**
It's important.	Es importante.	es eem-pour-**TAHN**-tay
It's serious.	Es grave.	es **GRA**-vay
It's possible.	Es posible	es po-**SEE**-blay
Like this?	¿Así?	ah-**SEE**
Maybe.	Quizás.	key-**SAHS**
Me, neither	Yo tampoco.	yo tam-**PO**-co
Me, too	Yo también.	yo tam-b-**N**
More or less	Más o menos.	mas oh **MAY**-nos
Really?	¿De veras?	day **VER**-ahs
Sure	¡Claro!	**CLA**-row
That depends.	Depende.	day-**PEN**-day
We'll see you.	Nos vemos.	nos **VAY**-mos

Para Practicar:

1. Name some phrases that could accompany "adiós": _____

   _____

2. Name a few words you could say when something is really great:

   _____

3. Name a few things you could say when things are going well:

   _____

Typing in Spanish with Microsoft Word
Inserting an International Character with Shortcut Keys

When you need to type letters with accent marks or use Spanish punctuation, you will use keys that you have probably never used before! Actually, you are *composing characters* using the **control** key. It is located on the bottom row of keys. You will see that it is such an important key that there is one on both sides. It keeps the computer from moving forward one space so that the accent goes on *top* of the letter instead of *beside* it.

Always remember to hold the control key down first. It will be the *key* to your success in word processing Spanish. With a little practice these keys will become a normal part of your word processing skills.

Also, if using MS Word, you may use the menu command Insert>Symbol.

To insert	Press
á, é, í, ó, ú, ý Á, É, Í, Ó, Ú, Ý	CTRL+' (APOSTROPHE), *the letter*
â, ê, î, ô, û Â, Ê, Î, Ô, Û	CTRL+SHIFT+^ (CARET), *the letter*
ã, ñ, õ Ã, Ñ, Õ	CTRL+SHIFT+~ (TILDE), *the letter*
ä, ë, ï, ö, ü, ÿ Ä, Ë, Ï, Ö, Ü, Ÿ	CTRL+SHIFT+: (COLON), *the letter*
¿	ALT+CTRL+SHIFT+?
¡	ALT+CTRL+SHIFT+!

Practicing What You Have Learned

Practice is an important part of the language learning process. The more you include practice in your daily routine, the more comfortable and fluent you will become. There is no easy way to practice. It just takes time. The key to practicing Spanish is to set realistic goals. Don't let the language learning process become overwhelming to you. Yes, there is a lot to learn, and it will take some time. But, by setting realistic goals, you have a greater chance of sticking with it. Each of us have different learning styles, so find out what works best for you and break the material down into small pieces. Some of us learn best by listening. Others need to write the words and phrases in order to visualize them. Generally the more of your senses that you involve in the learning process, the faster you will retain the information. So, focus and practice one thing at a time. It's doing the little things that will make the greatest difference in the long run. Working five minutes every day on your Spanish is **mucho** better than trying to put in an hour of practice time only once each week. Consistency in your practice is critical.

Here are some practice tips that have worked for me and others who have participated in *SpeakEasy's Survival Spanish*™ training programs over the last few years.

1. Start practicing first thing in the morning. The shower is a great place to start. Say the numbers or run through the months of the year while you wash your hair. If you practice when you start your day you are more likely to continue to practice as the day progresses.

2. Use your commute time to practice. Listening to CDs, music and Spanish language radio stations will help you get the rhythm of Spanish. It will also increase your vocabulary.

3. If you are stopped in traffic, look around you for numbers on billboards or the license tags of the cars in front of you to help you practice. Don't just sit there—do something!

4. Investigate sites on the internet. Sites such as www.about.spanish.com and www.studyspanish.com are great places to practice and to learn, not to mention the fact that they are free!

5. Buy Spanish magazines or pick up Spanish newspapers that are published in your area. Many magazines like *People* have Spanish versions and almost every community in the country has a Spanish language newspaper or two. Many of them are free.

6. If there aren't any Spanish newspapers in your area, you can find a variety of publications from Latin America online. Major cities in Latin America all have newspapers that are easy to find on-line.

7. Practice as often as possible; even five minutes a day will help.

8. Don't give up! You didn't learn English overnight and you won't learn Spanish that way either. Set realistic goals and don't go too far too fast.

9. Learn five to ten words each week.

10. Practice at work with a friend.

11. Read! These books will make great additions to your library.

    Baez, Francia and Chong, Nilda. *Latino Culture.* Intercultural Press, 2005

    Condon, John. *Good Neighbors.* Intercultural Press, 1997

    Einsohn, Marc and Steil, Gail. *The Idiot's Guide to Learning Spanish on Your Own.* Alpha Books, 1996

    Harvey, William. *Spanish for Human Resource Managers.* Barron's, 1997

    Hawson, Steven R. *Learn Spanish the Lazy Way.* Alpha Books, 1999.

    Kras, Eva. *Management in Two Cultures.* Intercultural Press, 1995.

    Reid, Elizabeth. Spanish *Lingo for the Savvy Gringo.* In One Ear Publications, 1997

    Wald, Susana. *Spanish for Dummies.* Wiley Publishing, 2000.

About the Author

Myelita Melton

Myelita Melton, founder of SpeakEasy Communications, remembers the first time she heard a "foreign" language. She knew from that moment what she wanted to do with her life. "Since I was always the kid in class that talked too much," Myelita says, "I figured it would be a good idea to learn more than one language- that way I could talk to a lot more people!" After high school, she studied in Mexico at the ***Instituto de Filológica Hispánica*** and completed both her BA and MA in French and Curriculum Design at Appalachian State University in Boone, NC. She has studied and speaks five languages: French, Spanish, Italian, German, and English.

"Lita's" unique career includes classroom instruction and challenging corporate experience. She has won several national awards, including a prestigious ***Rockefeller*** scholarship. In 1994 she was named to ***Who's Who Among Outstanding Americans***. Myelita's corporate experience includes owning a television production firm, working with NBC's Spanish news division, ***Canal de Noticias***, and Charlotte's PBS affiliate WTVI. In her spare time, she continues to broadcast with WDAV, a National Public Radio affiliate near Lake Norman in North Carolina where she lives.

In 1997 Myelita started SpeakEasy Communications to offer industry specific Spanish instruction in North Carolina. The company is now the nation's leader in Spanish training, offering over 30 ***SpeakEasy Spanish***™ programs and publications to companies, associations, and colleges throughout the US.

Lita is also a member of the National Speaker's Association and the National Council for Continuing Education and Training. Many of her clients say she is the most high-energy, results-oriented speaker they have ever seen. As she travels the country speaking on cultural diversity issues in the workplace and languages, she has truly realized her dream of being able to talk to the world.